Ninja® Foodi™ Pressure Cooker
MEAL PREP COOKBOOK

NINJA® Foodi™

PRESSURE COOKER

MEAL PREP
COOKBOOK

75 RECIPES
AND 8 WEEKS
OF PREP PLANS

MARLYNN JAYME SCHOTLAND

Photography by Hélène Dujardin

ROCKRIDGE
PRESS

For general information on our other products and services or to obtain technical support, please contact our Customer Care Department within the United States at (866) 744-2665, or outside the United States at (510) 253-0500.

Rockridge Press publishes its books in a variety of electronic and print formats. Some content that appears in print may not be available in electronic books, and vice versa.

Interior and Cover Designer: Diana Haas
Art Producer: Sue Bischofberger
Editor: Cecily McAndrews
Production Editor: Andrew Yackira
Production Manager: Martin Worthington

Photography © 2021 Hélène Dujardin, with food styling by Anna Hampton. Image of appliance on cover courtesy of SharkNinja Operating LLC.

ISBN: Print 978-1-64876-919-1 |
eBook 978-1-64876-262-8
R0

For Alain, Ethan, and Cate—my greatest loves and helpful taste testers!

CONTENTS

INTRODUCTION

I GREW UP IN A HOUSE THAT RAN ON THE MOTTO "COOKING IS LOVE." There was always someone in the kitchen—whether it was my mom, my dad, or my great-grandmother, Lola Epyon, who lived with us. Most of my memories as a child involve food—watching and learning tips and tricks from my family. From the time I was old enough to reach the kitchen counter, I knew the importance of an organized and well-prepped kitchen. After all, Filipino-style recipes usually call for upward of dozens of ingredients and require a lot of planning.

We didn't call it meal prepping back then, but that's exactly what it was. As a kid, I was taught to plan meals that used the same ingredients, prep ingredients ahead of time, and get creative with leftovers. In fact, one of my favorite kitchen games right now as a mom of two teenagers is to see what new delicious dish we can create from leftovers.

When I discovered the Ninja® Foodi™ Deluxe XL Pressure Cooker, I honestly couldn't believe how much easier this modern marvel made my life. I run my own business full time and raise two kids—plus a supercute, high-energy black Labrador retriever—so the time I spend in the kitchen HAS to be focused. Not only has the Ninja® Foodi™ helped me save time, it's also helped me step up my meal prepping game. And now, I'm excited to share some of my best tips and tricks with all of you.

Whether you're new to meal prepping or a pro at planning ahead, I hope you'll find your next favorite recipes in this cookbook. The 75 delicious recipes were written specifically for meal prepping with the Ninja® Foodi™ Deluxe XL Pressure Cooker, and most of them can be made in about 30 minutes and have 10 or fewer ingredients, making meal prep a breeze. I've included some of my family's favorite dishes, such as Crispy Paprika Chicken (page 150), Pasta with Bacon and Peas (page 174), and Butternut Squash Mac and Cheese (page 205). Not only are these meals delicious, but they also store and reheat well, making them perfect for meal prepping.

In this book, yummy, family-friendly recipes for breakfast, lunch, and dinner are organized into eight weeks of meal prep plans. Each plan comes with clear, easy-to-follow step-by-step instructions, as well as some fun bonus tips and ideas for leftovers. Once you get the hang of the process, feel free to use the meal plans as a guide. They are meant to be flexible so you can customize them to fit your own personal taste, budget, and schedule.

I wrote this book because I believe every home cook can find meal prep success in the kitchen. It's not about perfection; it's about learning some skills to help you make the most with what you have.

I hope you're ready to create some meal prep magic in your kitchen. I'll be with you every step of the way in this book, sharing helpful tips, tricks, substitutions, things to watch out for, and inspiration. Let's get started!

Black Bean Burrito Bowl, *page 210*

1

Ninja® Foodi™ Meal Prep Magic

WELCOME TO THE WONDERFUL WORLD OF MEAL PREP with the Ninja® Foodi™! Before you dive in and start making the recipes, I encourage you to read through this chapter carefully. You'll find lots of helpful tips and tricks to make the most of meal prepping with this amazing multi-cooker.

NO-PRESSURE MEAL PREP WITH THE FOODI™

My husband, two kids, and I sit down together for dinner every night. Between work, school, music lessons, and events, the days can get pretty hectic for all of us. Dinner is the one time of day when we can reconnect, catch up, and relax all together.

Trying to decide what to eat for dinner every night, on the other hand, can get stressful. Before I started meal prepping, I would waste so much mental and emotional energy trying to answer the dreaded "what's for dinner?" question. Then, I'd waste even *more* energy frantically trying to throw together a decent meal at the last minute—which would stress me out even more. Sound familiar?

That's where meal prep with the Ninja® Foodi™ comes in. This appliance has changed the way I cook for my family.

If you're new to the Ninja® Foodi™, have no fear—it's really easy to use. Once you learn how much you can do with this multi-cooker, you'll want to use it for all your cooking projects.

Because you can cook, crisp, bake, broil, and more in the Foodi™, it is a huge help in streamlining meal prep and planning. The Foodi™ is *made* for meal prepping. In just a few hours, I can prep, refrigerate, and freeze meals for most of the week!

Meal prepping is like a beautiful, well-orchestrated symphony—when the different components come together, it's kitchen magic. I've designed the meal plans in this book to be as simple as possible while still keeping the food flavorful and interesting. The step-by-step instructions will help you create five days' worth of food each week in a short amount of time.

If you have a busy household like I do, meal prep day is sanity-saving day. When you take the guesswork out of weeknight mealtimes, everything else seems a lot easier to manage.

Save Time

The Foodi™ cooks food beautifully and in less time than standard cooking methods. For instance, soups that normally take all day can pressure cook in an hour or less—without sacrificing any flavor. This allows you to prep more meals in less time. Most of the recipes in this book freeze and reheat well, which also saves you cooking time throughout the week.

Save Money

When you plan your meals and cook at home, you'll save money by not eating out as much. Those last-minute delivery dinners can add up. Plus, you save money by batch cooking and buying ingredients that can be used in more than one recipe. As you meal plan, you will also find that you are more aware of what ingredients you already have in stock in your pantry, refrigerator, and freezer, making you less likely to waste money on unnecessary duplicate purchases.

Maximize Kitchen Efficiency

The Ninja® Foodi™ is truly a magical multi-cooker that can do the work of several different appliances. In fact, it's the only kitchen tool you need for all the recipes in this book. With the Foodi™, you have fewer pots and pans to clean, which is always a huge plus in my book. It's truly the hardest-working tool in my kitchen, and it only takes up one corner of my kitchen counter.

Solve the "What's for Dinner?" Dilemma

As a mom, I know the pain of this question all too well. Meal prep and planning help alleviate the stress that can come with having to figure out what to cook after a long, hard day of work and school. During the busiest weeknights, it's nice to be able to walk into the kitchen and simply reheat a meal we prepped ahead of time. And, since everyone knows the game plan in advance, there tends to be less whining about what's on their plates.

Get Creative in the Kitchen

Meal prepping does not necessarily mean eating the same meals day after day. In fact, it can have quite the opposite effect on your weekly routine, helping you explore different recipes and combinations of flavors. You'll love learning how to use the same ingredients in totally different, delicious ways. The act of cooking is a nourishing, loving act that doesn't have to be a chore. I hope this book helps you discover new dishes that you love and inspires you to get creative in the kitchen.

FOODI™ PRESSURE COOKER 101

If you're new to the Foodi™, this next section will help you become familiar with the different functions and understand the appliance's many capabilities.

Parts and Programs

Pressure: This is the function used the most for recipes in this book. To pressure cook, you'll lock in the pressure lid and set the pressure valve to SEAL. After you set your temperature level, time, and select START/STOP to begin, liquid inside the pot forms steam, builds pressure, and cooks food at extremely high temperatures. This shortens cooking time and infuses moisture and flavor into the ingredients.

When the cook time is done, the Foodi™ will beep, display "Warm," and start counting down. Recipes will instruct you to either allow for natural release or quick release at this point. To let the pressure release naturally, simply leave the lid closed and sealed until the pressure valve goes down on its own. To do a quick release, carefully move the pressure release valve from SEAL to VENT. Warning: When you move the pressure release valve, hot steam will immediately vent out of the multi-cooker, so wear long oven mitts or use long tongs to avoid injury.

Air Crisp: Lock in the crisping lid, and your Ninja® Foodi™ acts like an air fryer or convection oven. Cook your food either in the Cook & Crisp™ basket or on the Deluxe Reversible Rack (both of which come with your Foodi™) for crispy, golden results without added fat.

Sear/Sauté: I love this function because it allows me to create truly one-pot dinners. Sauté meat right in the pot, then add the remaining ingredients to pressure cook or air crisp—no extra pan or stove top needed.

Steam: To steam food, you'll lock in the pressure lid and turn the knob over to VENT (as opposed to SEAL, as you do when pressure cooking). This setting is great for vegetables and fish.

THE NINJA® FOODI™

Pressure Release Valve
Easily release pressure.

Pressure Lid
Quickly tenderize and cook ingredients.

Reversible Rack
Use to steam, or reverse it to broil.

Cook & Crisp™ Basket
4-quart nonstick, ceramic-coated basket fits 3 lbs of French fries.

Crisping Lid
Use to finish off pressure cooked recipes or to air fry your food.

Cooking Pot
6.5-quart nonstick, ceramic-coated cooking pot, fits a 6-lb roast.

14 Levels of Safety
Passed rigorous testing to earn UL safety certification, giving you peace of mind.

Bake/Roast: Use this function for roasting veggies and casseroles and for baking cakes, pies, muffins, and more.

Broil: This setting distributes the highest heat from above and gives food a toasty, caramelized top.

Slow Cook/Yogurt: Cook food like stews and chilis at a lower temperature for a longer period of time. This setting also works to ferment milk to create homemade yogurt.

Dehydrate: Use this function to dehydrate fruit, veggies, and even meat to create yummy, healthy snacks.

Accessories

The Ninja® Foodi™ Deluxe XL Pressure Cooker & Air Fryer comes with everything you need to get started with most of the recipes in this cookbook (different retailers may have different packaging). You'll mostly be using the **inner pot, pressure lid, Cook & Crisp™ basket and diffuser**, the **Deluxe Reversible Rack**, and the **Ninja® Foodi™ silicone mitts**.

To expand your Foodi™ repertoire, consider buying these additional accessories:

Foodi™ All-Purpose Pans: Great to use for baking and air crisping desserts and food like the Loaded Vegetable Quiche (page 60).

Foodi™ Roasting Sling: This makes it easy to slide bulky items like baking pans and whole chickens in and out of the pot safely.

Extra Silicone Rings: Because the ring that comes with the Foodi™ can absorb the smell of cooked foods, you may want to have at least one extra ring on hand to swap in.

Foodi™ Mini Molds: These are great for cooking grab-and-go meals and snacks like Chorizo Egg Bites (page 82) and Lemon-Blueberry Mini Muffins (page 70).

Tips & Tricks

These pointers will help you make the most out of your Ninja®
Foodi™—and get great results every time you use the appliance:

- **When using the PRESSURE mode, make sure you add enough liquid.** You'll need at least 1 cup of water, broth, or sauce in most of the pressure cooked recipes in this book.

- If you are pressure cooking and then **finishing the food in the crisper**, be sure to remove any remaining liquid in the pot before crisping. This will ensure that your food gets nice and crispy.

- **When using the BAKE/ROAST function, lower the temperature by at least 25°F** from the temperature you would normally use for the same dish in a conventional oven.

- **Place your Foodi™ on a level surface, and make sure there is plenty of open space above the appliance.** Hot steam escapes when venting after pressure cooking, so I usually keep my Foodi™ on the kitchen island counter and not on a counter with cabinets above it.

Foodi™ Size & Scaling Down

Because of its larger size, the Ninja® Foodi™ 8-quart Deluxe XL Pressure Cooker & Air Fryer was used to develop the recipes in this cookbook. Each recipe in the chapters that follow makes at least 6 servings, with some going up to 10 servings.

If you have the original Ninja® Foodi™ pressure cooker, which has a 6½-quart capacity, some recipes may require a bit less cook time or fewer shakes of the Cook & Crisp™ basket. For best results, check the food's progress throughout cooking.

As a good rule of thumb, if you are using the original Foodi™ pressure cooker rather than the Deluxe XL Pressure Cooker & Air Fryer, you should scale down pressure-cooked recipes like soups, stews, and chilis by as much as 50 percent and place half as many ingredients in the basket. Whatever model you use, never add food above the fill line of the inner pot. If the ingredients reach or rise above the fill line, cook that dish in two batches.

FOODI™ MEAL PREP PRINCIPLES

Anyone can be successful at meal prep and planning. If you are just starting out, there are a few basic rules that can help make your meal prep experience with the Ninja® Foodi™ as efficient, safe, and tasty as possible. Once you get the hang of this multi-cooker, these principles will become routine. Then, you can learn what works best for you and create a process that makes the most sense for your schedule.

Keep It Simple

Meal prep is meant to make your life easier—not more complicated. That 15-step Filipino-style lumpia recipe with 20-plus ingredients handed down to me from my great-grandmother and mother makes for a fabulous, delicious meal—but it doesn't work for meal prepping.

In this cookbook, I kept meal prep newbies in mind, focusing on recipes that are made to be prepped ahead. The ingredients, recipes, and preparation steps are kept simple, and you'll find that with the Foodi™, even the most basic recipes are extra delicious and incredibly versatile.

Pick a Batch Cooking and Prep Day

Select a day each week as your meal prep day. You should allow a few hours to prep, cook, and store several meals.

For me, and for many others, Sunday is a great meal prep day. Not only do I have more free time to cook on Sundays, but I also find that the practice of prepping meals helps me prepare mentally for the week ahead. I do all of my chopping, slicing, dicing, and peeling in the morning while I watch my favorite cooking shows. Then, once all of my ingredients are prepped and organized, I spend the afternoon batch cooking. By dinner, I have a week's worth of meals for my family in the refrigerator and freezer.

Shopping Lists & Pantry Staples

Each of the meal plans in this cookbook includes full shopping lists for that week's recipes. Since many of the ingredients will be used in multiple recipes, the shopping lists contain the full quantity you will need of each ingredient to use in all of the recipes for that week's meal plan. Then, each recipe contains the specific amount needed to make that particular dish.

In the meal plans, ingredients are broken down by categories, similar to how they are organized in the grocery store. This makes it easy to shop more efficiently.

You'll also notice a few pantry staples that are repeated in many of the recipes throughout this book. See pages 14 and 15 for a list of oils, seasonings, and other basic ingredients to keep on hand for meal prepping success.

Storage

Storage plays an important role in meal prepping, so each recipe in this cookbook includes suggestions for how best to pack it up. Be sure to read the section on Storage Containers on page 14 before you get started.

Getting Creative with Leftovers

Meal prep does not mean eating the exact same thing over and over. Just because you cook four meals to enjoy throughout the week does not mean you have to eat them exactly the same way all week long. This is where you can really get creative and have fun.

Throughout the book, I share some of my favorite ways to reimagine leftovers. For example: Cheeseburger Pasta (page 182) leftovers are turned into Cheeseburger Pasta Soup. Both meals use the same ingredients, but they taste completely different.

Or, how about enjoying some steak and egg bites for breakfast using the Chorizo Egg Bites recipe (page 82) and substitute chorizo with leftover meat from Cheesesteaks (page 63)? Or making a cheesy short ribs pasta from leftover Kalbi (Korean-Style Beef Short Ribs, page 193) and Butternut Squash Mac and Cheese (page 205)?

By the time you've done a few weeks of meal prep, you'll no doubt have some of your own personal favorite leftover creations.

FOOD SAFETY

Food safety is always of the utmost importance in the kitchen. When it comes to meal prepping, there are certain guidelines to keep in mind for proper refrigerating, freezing, and reheating. These guidelines will help ensure that your efforts are not just delicious, but also safe and healthy.

Set Up Your Refrigerator and Freezer

First, check your cold storage temperatures. Your refrigerator should be set to a temperature at or below 40°F, and your freezer should be set to a temperature at or below 0°F. If you store food at higher temperatures than those, you run the risk of spoilage.

Next, organize your refrigerator and freezer. It's important to easily see what's inside—you don't want month-old leftovers hiding in the back and growing mold. I like to organize my refrigerator and freezer by categories. Everyone in our household is aware of where each type of food goes, so our refrigerator and freezer stay fairly easy to clean out and properly fill. This helps save money by preventing waste, and it makes meal planning even easier. One idea for keeping your meal prep food organized is to have part of one shelf in the refrigerator and part of one shelf in the freezer designated just for meal prep storage.

Finally, be sure to properly label and date each container. I've found it helps to place items on the shelf in the order that they are made.

Storing

Depending on the temperature of your kitchen, most food can safely remain on the kitchen counter for one to two hours.

On meal prep day, once you finish cooking a dish, portion it out into labeled storage containers. Allow the food to cool on your kitchen counter before placing it in the refrigerator. At the end of your meal prep day, you can shift items from the refrigerator to the freezer as needed.

It's important to allow food to cool down after cooking before storing it. Never place hot, just-cooked food in the refrigerator or freezer. This can encourage bacteria growth, which can make the food unsafe to eat.

Thawing and Reheating

With the Foodi™, you can cook and reheat food straight from the freezer without waiting for it to thaw. When cooking from frozen, use the PRESSURE function first to defrost and lock in the juices, then switch to the crisping lid and use the AIR CRISP function to reheat the outside of the food. When reheating meal-prepped food, you have several options:

To reheat pressure-cooked food in the Foodi™: Pour 1 cup of water into the inner pot, then place the food in a Foodi™ all-purpose pan on the Deluxe Reversible Rack. Then, select either PRESSURE or STEAM and set the timer for a few minutes to reheat. To reheat meaty pressure-cooked dishes, such as the Teriyaki Turkey Meatballs with Hoisin-Soy Glaze (page 156), place the food directly in the inner pot and use the SEAR/SAUTÉ function on HI for a few minutes.

To reheat air-crisped food in the Foodi™: Place the food in the Cook & Crisp™ basket, then use the AIR CRISP function at 350ºF to 375ºF and cook for 3 to 4 minutes.

To reheat a refrigerated meal in the microwave: Place the food in the microwave and reheat in 30-second increments until the food is completely thawed and heated to your liking. Most dishes are safely reheated when the internal temperature reads at least 165ºF on a food thermometer. For recipes that include rice or pasta, I find it's helpful to add a splash of water or stock to the dish before reheating. This prevents it from drying out.

Food Storage Guidelines

Knowing how long and at what temperature to refrigerate or freeze your meals is important for shopping and meal prepping. Use this chart to help you coordinate your grocery store trips, cooking days, and weekly meal plans.

ITEM	REFRIGERATOR	FREEZER
Salads (egg, chicken, ham, tuna, pasta)	3 to 5 days	Do not freeze
Casseroles with eggs	3 to 4 days	2 to 3 months
Bacon	1 week	1 month
Cooked sausage	1 week	1 to 2 months
Cooked ground meats	3 to 4 days	2 to 3 months
Soups and stews (with vegetables and/or meat)	3 to 4 days	2 to 3 months
Cooked chicken and fish	3 to 4 days	4 to 6 months
Steaks	3 to 5 days	6 to 12 months
Pizza	3 to 4 days	1 to 2 months

Source: FoodSafety.gov and FDA.gov

PREP YOUR KITCHEN

Though the Ninja® Foodi™ does the work of multiple appliances, there are a few additional kitchen tools that can help complete your meal prep experience.

Must-Have Equipment:

Chef's knife: A chef's knife is essential for safely slicing, dicing, and chopping fruits, vegetables, and meats. You don't need to spend a lot of money, and you certainly don't need a large set of several different types of knives. Start with one good chef's knife, and you'll be set.

Measuring cups and spoons: Using correct measurements helps ensure that you'll get flavorful, consistent results every time you follow your favorite recipes.

Cutting board: Whether you like plastic, bamboo, or wooden cutting boards, you'll need at least one of them for prepping ingredients. It's best if you have at least two—one to use for meat only, and another for fruits, vegetables, and other foods. That way, you can avoid cross-contaminating fruits and vegetables with raw meat.

Nice-to-Have Equipment:

Meat thermometer: Use a digital instant-read food thermometer to take the guesswork out of cooking meat and reheating leftovers.

Whisks: These are great for whisking eggs, salad dressing, sauces, and dry ingredients for baked goods. A fork will work in a pinch, but I find a whisk results in better distribution and consistency.

Silicone spatula or wooden spoon: A heatproof silicone spatula makes it easy to scramble eggs and safely scrape all of that delicious food out of the cooking pot. You can also use a wooden spoon.

Baking pans: Baking pans and dishes are not only great for baking delicious desserts in the Foodi™, but also are ideal for cooking savory foods, such as the Sausage and Spinach Frittata (page 122).

Storage Containers

Storage is a crucial step in meal prepping, and there are several storage options to consider.

Glass: My favorite storage containers are made of glass. They're easy to clean (very important), they don't tend to hold lingering food smells like other containers can, and they tend to be dishwasher-, microwave-, and freezer-safe. I buy these types of containers in multiple sizes, both rectangular and round. The downsides of glass containers: They are heavier and take up more space than other container options, they're breakable, and they can be expensive.

Plastic: Plastic is lighter and less expensive than glass, and most plastic containers are microwave-, freezer-, and dishwasher-safe. The downsides of plastic containers: They tend to absorb food smells and flavors, and it can be tricky to clean them thoroughly.

Reusable Storage Bags: Nowadays, many different companies sell food-grade reusable silicone bags. I like them because they're durable and better for the planet. Plus, they're fantastic for storing soups, chilis, vegetables, and flat cuts of meat such as chicken breasts. Once the contents of the bags are fully frozen, you can stack them, which really allows you to maximize room in the refrigerator and freezer. Make sure you buy bags specifically labeled "food grade." You can also use heavy-duty zip-top freezer bags, though they are not reusable.

Other Containers: Mason jars can hold homemade sauces, granola, dressings, and dips. You can also use large aluminum foil pans for casseroles and baked dishes.

Pantry Staples

The following pantry items are used frequently throughout the book. For easy meal prepping, keep them stocked in your kitchen at all times.

- Extra-virgin olive oil
- Nonstick cooking spray

- Broth or stock (chicken, vegetable, and/or beef)
- Canned tomatoes (diced, stewed, and crushed)
- Kosher salt and freshly ground black pepper
- Dried herbs (especially thyme, oregano, basil, and parsley)
- Ground spices (especially paprika, cinnamon, cumin, ginger, chili powder, garlic powder, and onion powder)
- All-purpose flour
- Granulated sugar

Shopping for Fresh Ingredients

In my decades of cooking and baking, I've found that the most delicious dishes start with the best ingredients. This means using the freshest ingredients when they are at their seasonal best. For example, strawberries are sweetest during their peak in summer, and wild mushrooms usually have their fullest, richest flavor in the fall.

Most of the recipes in this cookbook call for ingredients that can be found year-round. However, a few ingredients may be seasonal where you live. If you can't find an ingredient because it's off-season, the next best bet is to buy it frozen. Frozen fruits and veggies are usually picked at their ripest and then flash frozen immediately after to preserve their freshness and flavor.

ABOUT THE RECIPES

These recipes focus on simplicity and speed—two key components of meal prep and planning—without sacrificing flavor. Most recipes require 10 or fewer easy-to-find ingredients. Plus, almost all of the recipes have a cook time of 30 minutes or less.

I also wanted to be sure the meal plans included recipes that used similar ingredients, since the point of meal prepping is to help save money and time. These recipes can also easily be reinvented into different leftover meals; I've noted some of my favorite creative leftover ideas throughout the book

There are two important additional elements included with each recipe: Recipe Labels and Recipe Tips.

Recipe Labels

Dairy-Free: These recipes do not contain milk, cheese, cream, butter, or other dairy products.

Gluten-Free: Gluten is found in many grains, including wheat and barley. Recipes labeled Gluten-Free do not have any ingredients that contain these grains.

One and Done: These recipes require one step of either pressure cooking or air crisping—no preheating, sautéing, or other pre-cooking. Just combine the ingredients in the Foodi™, select the function, and wait for delicious results.

Ready to Go: These recipes include ingredients that can be prepped ahead of time and stored in containers for several days before cooking. When you're ready to cook, take out the prepped ingredients and prepare them according to the recipe directions.

Under 30 Minutes: These recipes require less than 30 minutes of hands-on cooking time.

Vegetarian: These are recipes that do not contain meat or seafood. Vegan suggestions (without dairy, honey, or other animal products) are offered in some recipes.

Recipe Tips

Ready to Go: Instructions that indicate when to add prepped ingredients in the recipe.

Prep Tips: Tips and tricks for handling and/or preparing specific ingredients in the recipe.

Variation Tips: Easy ingredient swaps for adding a twist to recipes or using what you have in your kitchen.

Storage: Instructions for how best to store the food for freshness, safety, and best flavor.

2

The Prep Plans

TO HELP YOU GET STARTED, I'VE CREATED EIGHT WEEKS OF
meal plans. Each plan contains three or four recipes made completely in the Foodi™, along with a shopping list, step-by-step instructions to guide you on meal prep day, and a weekly plan with suggestions for how to enjoy leftovers.

MAKING SENSE OF MEAL PREPPING

The following meal plans are here to help you get started on your own meal prep and planning journey using the Foodi™. As you cook through Weeks 1 through 8, make note of what works and doesn't work for you. Then, you can take that knowledge and create meal plans centered around your own taste preferences as well as your particular schedule and budget.

Here are some additional tips to help you as you make your own meal plans:

One of the easiest ways to start with meal prep is to **group recipes that contain similar ingredients**. This way, you can prep and cook batches of those ingredients at the same time. Common ingredients to group together are meats, vegetables and aromatics (onions, garlic, ginger), and fresh herbs. For example, Sausage and Spinach Frittata (page 122) goes well with Lasagna Soup (page 142) and Italian Sausage Pasta (page 184). All three recipes can be cooked with sausage, and all contain onions, garlic, and spinach.

You can also have fun by **mixing and matching meal components** to create new and interesting meals throughout the week. For example, make the Popcorn Chicken (page 39) and enjoy it with a side of fries one night, then enjoy it over Butternut Squash Mac and Cheese (page 205) on another night, and serve the rest with Mexican-Style Street Corn (page 201) for lunch another day.

Finally, think about **staple recipes that offer *a lot* of potential variety in the ways you serve them**—recipes like Classic Beef Tacos (page 178) and Tequila, Lime, and Chipotle Shrimp Tacos (page 77). With the meat from either recipe, you can make so much more than just tacos. Turn the beef or shrimp into a breakfast hash with eggs and potatoes. Or, make a large lunch salad with mixed greens, corn, black beans, and sliced avocado. Both the beef and the shrimp would be delicious served with rice and sautéed vegetables, or even turned into a soup when heated with some stock, cream, and refrigerated tortellini.

Although the weekly meal plans here mostly call for refrigerating the dishes and eating them throughout the week, all the recipes in this cookbook are freezer friendly. That means you can stock up on options to break out if you are stuck in a mealtime rut or feel like going off plan. And, if you are feeding more people, you can always defrost multiple servings.

Meal prep is an opportunity for you to flex your creative muscles. Don't forget to write a shopping list, similar to the ones used in this book, to keep you on track and organized.

WEEK 1: EVERYTHING'S BETTER WITH BACON

So many great meals start with the sizzle and salty crunch of bacon. And if you're new to the Foodi™, bacon is one of the best first foods to learn how to air crisp. This week's menu is full of satisfying dishes that prove that everything really is better with bacon.

SHOPPING LIST

Check your pantry for: nonstick cooking spray, chicken broth, cornstarch, soy sauce, kosher salt, black pepper, dried thyme, and dried oregano.

VEGETABLES, HERBS, SPICES

- 3 pounds Yukon Gold or russet potatoes
- 6 medium carrots
- 2 celery stalks
- 3 scallions (optional)
- 2 small yellow onions
- 6 garlic cloves

PROTEIN

- 1 pound boneless, skinless chicken breasts
- 21 slices bacon
- 8 large eggs

GRAINS

- 6 English muffins
- 2 cups white rice

DAIRY

- 2 cups heavy (whipping) cream
- ½ cup sour cream
- 1 tablespoon milk (2%, 1%, or skim)
- 1 tablespoon unsalted butter
- 8 ounces cream cheese
- 6 slices cheddar cheese
- 2½ cups shredded cheddar cheese

FROZEN

- 1 cup frozen peas
- 1 cup frozen corn kernels

OTHER

- 12 ounces penne pasta
- 1 package powdered ranch seasoning

MEAL PREP MENU

	BREAKFAST	LUNCH	DINNER
Day 1	Bacon and Egg Breakfast Sandwiches	Loaded Baked Potato Soup	Chicken, Bacon, and Ranch Pasta
Day 2	Bacon and Egg Breakfast Sandwiches	Fried Rice	Loaded Baked Potato Soup
Day 3	Bacon and Egg Breakfast Sandwiches	Chicken, Bacon, and Ranch Pasta	Fried Rice
Day 4	Bacon and Egg Breakfast Sandwiches	Loaded Baked Potato Soup	Chicken, Bacon, and Ranch Pasta
Day 5	Bacon and Egg Breakfast Sandwiches	Loaded Baked Potato Soup	Fried Rice

STEP-BY-STEP PREP

1. Fully prepare the **Bacon and Egg Breakfast Sandwiches** (page 25). While the sandwiches are crisping, chop 15 slices of bacon and set aside. When the sandwiches are done cooking, let them cool completely at room temperature, then wrap them in aluminum foil, label, and refrigerate. Wash the pot and wipe it dry.

2. Select SEAR/SAUTÉ, set the temperature to HI, and select START/STOP to begin. Let the Foodi™ preheat for 5 minutes.

3. Meanwhile, chop the carrots, dice the onions, and mince the garlic for the **Fried Rice** (page 27) and **Loaded Baked Potato Soup** (page 29). Chop the celery for the **Loaded Baked Potato Soup**. Divide the veggies according to recipe measurements for the remaining three recipes.

4. Add the bacon you chopped in step 1 to the pot. Sauté for 5 to 6 minutes, just until the bacon is cooked, and then divide the bacon evenly among three bowls for the remaining three recipes.

5. Prepare the **Fried Rice,** continuing with steps 3 through 10 on pages 27 and 28.

6. While the fried rice is cooking, peel and chop the potatoes for the **Loaded Baked Potato Soup**. When the rice is done cooking, portion it out into containers, let it cool to room temperature, then label and refrigerate and/or freeze.

7. Select SEAR/SAUTÉ on your Foodi™, set the temperature to HI, and select START/STOP to begin. Heat 2 tablespoons of extra-virgin olive oil in the Foodi™ pot, and use a wooden spoon to scrape up any browned bits that remain from the Fried Rice. Then, continue preparing the **Loaded Baked Potato Soup** (starting with step 3 on page 29).

8. While the soup is pressure cooking, chop the chicken for the **Chicken, Bacon, and Ranch Pasta** (page 31), and measure out the remaining ingredients (pasta through cheddar cheese).

9. When the soup is done cooking, let it cool to room temperature. Then, portion the soup into containers, label, and refrigerate or freeze. Wash the Foodi™ pot and wipe it dry.

10. Finish preparing the **Chicken, Bacon, and Ranch Pasta** (steps 3 through 8 on pages 31 and 32). When cooking is complete, let the pasta cool completely at room temperature, then portion it out into containers, label, and refrigerate or freeze.

Bacon and Egg Breakfast Sandwiches

SERVES 6

I love incorporating these grab-and-go breakfast sandwiches into my meal plans. It's so nice to have a hearty, full breakfast ready each morning. The Foodi™ crisps up bacon beautifully, and the inner pot helps you make fluffy scrambled eggs—with easy cleanup! On days when you want a lighter breakfast, you can still enjoy these for lunch or as breakfast-for-dinner.

NUT-FREE, UNDER 30 MINUTES

PREP TIME: 5 minutes
TOTAL COOK TIME: 17 minutes

AIR CRISP: 10 minutes + 3 minutes at 400°F

SAUTÉ: 4 minutes

ACCESSORIES: Deluxe Reversible Rack

STORAGE: Store in an airtight container in the refrigerator for up to 4 days or in the freezer for up to 2 months. To reheat in the Foodi™, air crisp at 350°F for 2 minutes.

6 slices bacon
6 large eggs
1 tablespoon milk
1 tablespoon unsalted butter
6 English muffins, split
6 slices cheddar cheese

1. Place the Deluxe Reversible Rack in the higher broil position, and drape the bacon over the rack. Lower the rack into the inner pot of your Ninja® Foodi™.

2. Close the crisping lid. Select AIR CRISP, set the temperature to 400°F, and set the time to 10 minutes. Select START/STOP to begin.

3. Meanwhile, in a large bowl, beat the eggs with the milk until smooth.

4. When the bacon has finished cooking, lift the crisping lid and remove the rack from the unit. Set the bacon aside to cool. Rinse out any bacon drippings in the pot, wipe the pot dry, and put it back in the unit.

5. Select SEAR/SAUTÉ and set the temperature to HI. Place the butter in the inner pot, let it melt, and then pour in the eggs. Using a wooden spoon, continuously stir the eggs until they are fully cooked and scrambled, 2 to 4 minutes. Transfer the eggs to a plate. Once the pot has cooled a bit, wipe the inside clean with a paper towel.

6. To assemble the sandwiches: Set the English muffins out on a clean work surface. Divide the scrambled eggs among the bottom halves of the muffins, then top each mound of eggs with one slice of bacon (I break or fold the bacon in half to cover more area in the sandwich) and one slice of cheese. Place a muffin top on each sandwich then poke a toothpick through the center of each sandwich to hold it together. Place the Deluxe Reversible Rack in the lower steam position without the Deluxe Layer installed and lower the rack into the Foodi™ pot. Place 3 of the sandwiches on the rack. Next, install the Deluxe Layer on the rack and place the remaining sandwiches on it.

7. Select AIR CRISP, set the temperature to 400ºF, and set the time to 3 minutes. Select START/STOP to begin.

8. When cooking is complete, carefully remove the rack from the pot and allow the sandwiches to cool for a minute if you are serving them immediately. If you'll be eating these later for meal planning, allow the sandwiches to cool at room temperature, then place each sandwich in an airtight container and refrigerate or freeze.

Per serving: Calories: 385; Total fat: 21g; Saturated fat: 10g; Cholesterol: 231mg; Sodium: 648mg; Carbohydrates: 27g; Fiber: 3g; Protein: 22g

Fried Rice

I grew up eating some version of fried rice almost every day, so I'm well-versed in just how much this dish is made for meal planning. Enjoy it for lunch or dinner on its own—with protein, grains, and veggies, it's a delicious one-pot meal. You could also enjoy this as a side dish with Filipino-Style Chicken Adobo (page 148) or Lightened-Up Orange Chicken (page 99). For breakfast, serve it with an over-easy egg and sliced avocado.

NUT-FREE

PREP TIME: 10 minutes
TOTAL COOK TIME:
29 minutes

APPROX. PRESSURE BUILD: 10 minutes
PRESSURE COOK:
4 minutes
PRESSURE RELEASE:
natural for 5, then quick

SAUTÉ: 10 minutes

STORAGE: Store in airtight containers in the refrigerator for up to 4 days or in the freezer for up to 3 months.

5 slices bacon, chopped

3 medium carrots, chopped

1 small onion, diced

2 garlic cloves, minced

½ teaspoon kosher salt

¼ teaspoon freshly ground black pepper

2 cups white rice

1 (14.5-ounce) can chicken broth

¼ cup soy sauce

1 cup frozen peas

2 large eggs, lightly beaten

1. Select SEAR/SAUTÉ on your Ninja® Foodi™ and set the temperature to HI. Select START/STOP to begin. Let the Foodi™ preheat for 5 minutes.

2. Place the bacon in the inner pot and sauté for 4 to 5 minutes, until cooked through. Using a slotted spoon, transfer the bacon to a paper towel–lined plate and set aside.

3. Add the carrots, onion, garlic, salt, and pepper to the pot and sauté for 2 to 3 minutes, just until the vegetables are soft and fragrant. Select START/STOP.

4. Pour the rice on top of the vegetables in an even layer. Stir in the chicken broth and soy sauce.

CONTINUED ▶

5. Assemble the pressure lid, making sure the pressure release valve is in the SEAL position. Select PRESSURE and set it to HI. Set the time to 4 minutes. Select START/STOP to begin.

6. When the pressure cooking is complete, allow the pressure to release naturally for 5 minutes. After 5 minutes, quick release the remaining pressure by moving the pressure release valve to the VENT position. Carefully remove the lid when the unit has finished releasing the pressure.

7. Select SEAR/SAUTÉ and set the temperature to HI. Select START/STOP to begin.

8. Immediately stir in the peas until well combined.

9. Using a wooden spoon, scrape the rice to the sides of the pot to create a well in the middle. Pour the eggs into the well and scramble, stirring continuously for 2 to 3 minutes, just until the eggs are fully cooked. Break up the eggs with the wooden spoon and stir all ingredients to combine.

10. Let the fried rice cool to room temperature, then portion it into individual containers and refrigerate or freeze.

Per serving: *Calories: 358; Total fat: 7g; Saturated fat: 2g; Cholesterol: 69mg; Sodium: 727mg; Carbohydrates: 61g; Fiber: 3g; Protein: 11g*

Loaded Baked Potato Soup

Loaded baked potatoes with all the fixings are a comfort food staple. The Foodi™ turns this delectable dish into a cozy, chunky, hearty soup. Enjoy it as it is, or, if you prefer a creamy soup, use an immersion (hand) blender to puree the ingredients in the pot at the end. Serve the soup with a big salad, slices of sourdough bread, or a sandwich.

NUT-FREE

PREP TIME: 15 minutes
TOTAL COOK TIME:
35 minutes

APPROX. PRESSURE BUILD: 10 minutes
PRESSURE COOK:
10 minutes
PRESSURE RELEASE:
natural for 5 minutes, then quick

SAUTÉ: 10 minutes

STORAGE: Store in an airtight container in the refrigerator for up to 4 days or in the freezer for up to 2 months.

5 slices bacon, chopped

3 medium carrots, chopped

2 celery stalks, chopped

1 cup frozen corn kernels, thawed

1 small yellow onion, diced

4 garlic cloves, minced

½ teaspoon dried thyme

½ teaspoon dried oregano

3 pounds Yukon Gold or russet potatoes, peeled and cut into 1-inch cubes

3 tablespoons cornstarch

4 cups (1 quart) chicken broth

1 cup heavy (whipping) cream (or milk)

½ teaspoon kosher salt

¼ teaspoon freshly ground black pepper

½ cup sour cream

½ cup shredded cheddar cheese

3 scallions, thinly sliced (optional)

1. Select SEAR/SAUTÉ on your Ninja® Foodi™ and set the temperature to HI. Select START/STOP to begin. Let the Foodi™ preheat for 5 minutes.

2. Add the bacon and sauté until it is cooked through, 4 to 5 minutes. Using a slotted spoon, transfer the bacon to a paper towel–lined plate and set aside.

3. Add the carrots, celery, corn, onion, garlic, thyme, and oregano to the pot and sauté, stirring constantly, for 3 to 5 minutes, until the vegetables are soft and fragrant.

4. Stir in the potatoes. Sprinkle the cornstarch over the vegetables and stir to coat well. Select START/STOP.

CONTINUED ▶

5. Pour in the broth, heavy cream, salt, and pepper. Stir to combine.

6. Assemble the pressure lid, making sure the pressure release valve is in the SEAL position. Select PRESSURE and set it to HI. Set the time to 10 minutes. Select START/ STOP to begin.

7. When the pressure cooking is complete, allow the pressure to release naturally for 5 minutes. After 5 minutes, quick release the remaining pressure by moving the pressure release valve to the VENT position. Carefully remove the lid when the unit has finished releasing the pressure.

8. Immediately stir in the sour cream, cheddar cheese, and bacon. Garnish with scallions, if using.

9. Let the soup cool to room temperature, then portion it into individual containers and refrigerate or freeze.

Per serving: *Calories: 499; Total fat: 25g; Saturated fat: 14g; Cholesterol: 81mg; Sodium: 998mg; Carbohydrates: 58g; Fiber: 7g; Protein: 12g*

Chicken, Bacon, and Ranch Pasta

This cheesy, slightly tangy pasta has a decadent, bacony crunch, making for a truly satisfying meal—with lots of leftovers. To mix things up when enjoying leftovers, consider adding your favorite vegetables to this dish. When reheating, simply mix in an additional tablespoon of water and a handful of chopped broccoli florets, spinach, or frozen peas. The veggies will steam while the pasta is reheating. Then, stir to combine all the flavors before eating.

NUT-FREE

PREP TIME: 5 minutes
TOTAL COOK TIME:
27 minutes

APPROX. PRESSURE
BUILD: 10 minutes
PRESSURE COOK:
4 minutes
PRESSURE RELEASE:
natural for 5 minutes,
then quick

SAUTÉ: 8 minutes

5 slices bacon, chopped

1 pound boneless, skinless chicken breasts, cut into bite-size chunks

½ teaspoon kosher salt

¼ teaspoon freshly ground black pepper

2 (14.5-ounce) cans low-sodium chicken broth

1 cup heavy (whipping) cream

1 (1-ounce) package powdered ranch seasoning

1 (8-ounce) package cream cheese

12 ounces penne pasta

2 cups shredded cheddar cheese

1. Select SEAR/SAUTÉ on your Ninja® Foodi™ and set the temperature to HI. Select START/STOP to begin.

2. Place the bacon in the Foodi™ pot and sauté for about 4 minutes, until it is cooked to your preferred crispiness. Using a slotted spoon, transfer the bacon to a paper towel–lined plate and set aside.

3. Season the chicken with the salt and pepper and place it in the pot. Sauté for 4 to 5 minutes, just until lightly browned on all sides. Select START/STOP.

4. Pour the chicken broth into the pot. Using a wooden spoon, scrape up any browned bits left from the bacon. Stir in the cream and ranch seasoning.

CONTINUED ▶

Chicken, Bacon, and Ranch Pasta continued

STORAGE: Store in an airtight container in the refrigerator for up to 4 days or in the freezer for up to 2 months. To reheat in the Foodi™, select SEAR/SAUTÉ, set the temperature to HI, and select START/STOP to begin. Heat 1 tablespoon of olive oil, then place the leftovers in the pot. Add 1 tablespoon of water and stir until fully reheated. To reheat in the microwave, place one serving in a microwave-safe bowl and add 1 tablespoon of water or milk. Microwave in 45-second increments until fully reheated.

5. Place the pasta in the pot, and gently push down the noodles so most are submerged in the liquid.

6. Assemble the pressure lid, making sure the pressure release valve is in the SEAL position. Select PRESSURE and set it to HI. Set the time to 4 minutes. Select START/STOP to begin.

7. When the pressure cooking is complete, allow the pressure to release naturally for 5 minutes. After 5 minutes, quick release the remaining pressure by moving the pressure release valve to the VENT position. Carefully remove the lid when the unit has finished releasing the pressure.

8. Stir in the cream cheese and cheddar cheese until they have melted into the sauce. Let the pasta cool at room temperature, then portion the pasta into individual containers for the week. Top each serving with cooked bacon bits before refrigerating or freezing.

Per serving: Calories: 779; Total fat: 48g; Saturated fat: 25g; Cholesterol: 189mg; Sodium: 825mg; Carbohydrates: 47g; Fiber: 2g; Protein: 40g

WEEK 2: COMFORT FOOD CLASSICS

Comfort food is timeless, featuring flavors and ingredients that remain popular generation after generation. It's food that warms us up from the inside out, reminding us of home, and it's the food we reach for after a long day. This week, we're putting the Foodi™ spin on some comfort food classics to enjoy all week long.

SHOPPING LIST

Check your pantry for: nonstick cooking spray, extra-virgin olive oil, vegetable or chicken broth, beef broth, kosher salt, black pepper, dried oregano, paprika, cinnamon, light brown sugar, and all-purpose flour.

VEGETABLES, HERBS, AND SPICES

- 2 medium carrots
- 2 celery stalks
- 2 small yellow onions
- 5 garlic cloves
- 2 tablespoons chopped fresh parsley
- 2 tablespoons fresh chopped basil
- Salad greens

PROTEIN

- 2 pounds chicken breast tenders
- 1 pound 80% lean ground beef

GRAINS AND NOODLES

- 12 slices sourdough (or other) bread
- 1½ cups steel-cut oats
- 1 large hoagie roll
- 12 ounces spaghetti

DAIRY

- 2½ cups milk (2%, whole, or 1%)
- ¼ cup half-and-half
- 12 slices cheddar cheese
- 6 slices provolone cheese
- Grated Parmesan cheese (optional)

OTHER

- 4 (15-ounce) cans crushed tomatoes
- 2 tablespoons tomato paste
- ¼ cup smooth peanut butter
- ¼ cup jam or jelly
- ¾ cup mayonnaise
- 2 tablespoons coconut oil
- ½ cup red wine
- Dipping sauces (such as ketchup, honey mustard, or ranch)

MEAL PREP MENU

	BREAKFAST	LUNCH	DINNER
Day 1	PB&J Oatmeal	Grilled Cheese and Tomato Soup	Popcorn Chicken
Day 2	PB&J Oatmeal	Popcorn Chicken served over salad	Beef Ragù with Spaghetti
Day 3	PB&J Oatmeal	Beef Ragù with Spaghetti	Grilled Cheese and Tomato Soup
Day 4	PB&J Oatmeal	Grilled Cheese and Tomato Soup	Beef Ragù with Spaghetti
Day 5	PB&J Oatmeal	Grilled Cheese and Tomato Soup	Popcorn Chicken served in hoagie rolls

STEP-BY-STEP PREP

1. Prepare step 1 of the **Popcorn Chicken** (page 39).

2. Prepare the **PB&J Oatmeal** (page 36), steps 1 through 4.

3. While the oatmeal is cooking, dice the onions and mince the garlic. Divide into separate bowls for the **Grilled Cheese and Tomato Soup** (page 41) and the **Beef Ragù with Spaghetti** (page 44).

4. When the oatmeal is done cooking, continue with steps 5 and 6 of the recipe. Portion the finished oatmeal into containers, and let cool slightly at room temperature. Label, then refrigerate. Wash and dry the Foodi™ pot.

5. Prepare the **Popcorn Chicken**, steps 2 through 6.

6. While the chicken is cooking, chop the carrots and celery for the **Beef Ragù with Spaghetti**.

7. When the chicken is done cooking, let it cool slightly at room temperature. Portion the chicken into containers, label, and refrigerate or freeze. Wash and dry the Foodi™ pot.

8. Fully prepare the **Grilled Cheese and Tomato Soup**. Let the sandwiches and soup cool completely at room temperature. Wrap the sandwiches in aluminum foil and portion the soup into containers. Label all, then refrigerate. Wash the Foodi™ pot, then wipe it dry.

9. Fully prepare the **Beef Ragù with Spaghetti**. Let it cool completely at room temperature, then portion it into containers, label, and refrigerate or freeze.

PB&J Oatmeal

One of the ways to keep meal planning fun (no boring meals) is to combine a dish that's normally enjoyed for one meal of the day with a dish that's typically enjoyed for another meal of the day. Take this peanut butter and jelly oatmeal. Here, you're combining a warm, soothing breakfast with a timeless lunch classic.

VEGETARIAN

PREP TIME: 5 minutes
TOTAL COOK TIME:
27 minutes

**APPROX. PRESSURE
BUILD:** 10 minutes
PRESSURE COOK:
7 minutes
PRESSURE RELEASE:
natural for 10 minutes,
then quick

VARIATION TIP: Try this with different toppings throughout the week. Some ideas include sliced almonds, strawberries, and bananas, plus mini chocolate chips and chopped peanuts.

2 tablespoons coconut oil
1½ cups steel-cut oats
3 cups water
½ cup milk
1 teaspoon cinnamon

2 tablespoons packed
 light brown sugar
¼ cup smooth
 peanut butter
¼ cup jam or jelly,
 for serving

1. Select SEAR/SAUTÉ on your Ninja® Foodi™, set the temperature to HI, and select START/STOP to begin. Let the Foodi™ preheat for 5 minutes.

2. Add the coconut oil to the pot. Once the oil has melted, add the oats. Sauté until lightly toasted, 2 to 3 minutes.

3. Pour the water, milk, and cinnamon into the pot. Using a wooden spoon, stir to combine the ingredients and scrape up any browned bits at the bottom of the pot.

4. Assemble the pressure lid, making sure the pressure release valve is in the SEAL position. Select PRESSURE and set it to HI. Set the time to 7 minutes. Select START/STOP to begin.

5. When the pressure cooking is complete, allow the pressure to release naturally for 10 minutes. After 10 minutes, quick release the remaining pressure by moving the pressure release valve to the VENT position. Carefully remove the lid when the unit has finished releasing pressure.

6. Immediately stir in the brown sugar and peanut butter. Let the oatmeal cool to room temperature, then divide it among airtight containers, label, and refrigerate.

7. When ready to serve, reheat and top each serving with a dollop of jam or jelly.

Per serving: *Calories: 341; Total fat: 15g; Saturated fat: 6g; Cholesterol: 2mg; Sodium: 16mg; Carbohydrates: 48g; Fiber: 5g; Protein: 7g*

STORAGE: Refrigerate in an airtight container for up to 1 week. To reheat in the Foodi™, add 1 tablespoon of milk to the pot. Select SEAR/SAUTÉ, set the temperature to HI, and select START/STOP to begin. Heat until warmed through. To reheat in the microwave, measure out your serving into a microwave-safe bowl, pour in 1 tablespoon of water or milk, and microwave for 45 seconds to 1 minute. Stir and enjoy.

Popcorn Chicken

Healthier than fast-food versions, thanks to the Foodi™'s AIR CRISP function, this popcorn chicken is on regular rotation in my house. We like to serve it with fries and salad, but it's also a fun topping for Butternut Squash Mac and Cheese (page 205). Or, scoop the chicken into hoagie rolls for popcorn chicken sandwiches. This is a great meal plan recipe, since it's easy to portion out. It's also fun to serve for a game day get-together.

NUT-FREE

PREP TIME: 10 minutes, plus 15 minutes to marinate
TOTAL COOK TIME: 20 minutes

AIR CRISP: 10 minutes at 370°F per batch

ACCESSORIES: Cook & Crisp™ basket

STORAGE: Store in an airtight container in the refrigerator for up to 4 days or in the freezer for up to 3 months.

- 2 pounds chicken breast tenders, cut into 1-inch pieces
- 2 cups milk
- 2½ teaspoon paprika, divided
- 3 teaspoons kosher salt, divided
- 2½ teaspoons freshly ground black pepper, divided
- 3 cups all-purpose flour
- Nonstick cooking spray
- Dipping sauces for serving, such as ranch, honey mustard, or ketchup
- Salad greens, for serving
- 1 large hoagie roll, for serving

1. In a large bowl, combine the chicken, milk, ½ teaspoon of paprika, 1 teaspoon salt, and ½ teaspoon pepper. Cover and refrigerate for at least 15 minutes or up to 6 hours.

2. In a large shallow bowl, whisk together the flour and remaining 2 teaspoons of paprika, 2 teaspoons of salt, and 2 teaspoons of black pepper.

CONTINUED ▶

3. Remove the chicken from the marinade, but keep the bowl with the marinade. Working in small batches, dredge the chicken in the flour mixture. Shake off the excess flour, then dunk the chicken briefly in the marinade. Dredge the chicken for a second time in the dry ingredients, fully coating each piece of chicken. Gently shake off the excess flour. Place the coated chicken pieces on a plate while you repeat this step with the remaining chicken.

4. Spray the bottom and sides of the Cook & Crisp™ basket with the cooking spray. Working in batches, place an even layer of coated chicken pieces in the bottom of the basket. Set aside the rest of the chicken. Spray the top of the chicken pieces with cooking spray, then lower the basket into the inner pot of your Ninja® Foodi™.

5. Select AIR CRISP, set the temperature to 370°F, and set the time to 10 minutes. Select START/STOP to begin. After 5 minutes, remove the basket and gently shake it to toss the chicken. Return the basket to the pot, close the lid, and cook for 5 more minutes.

6. Cooking is complete when the internal temperature of the chicken reads at least 165°F on a food thermometer and the chicken reaches your desired level of crispiness. When cooking is complete, lift out the basket and transfer the chicken to a plate. Repeat steps 4 and 5 until all the chicken pieces are cooked.

7. Let the chicken pieces cool at room temperature, then portion them into individual containers for the week, along with small containers of dipping sauces. Place salad greens in one of those containers for lunch on day 2, and place a hoagie roll in another for dinner on day 5.

Per serving: Calories: 277; Total fat: 4g; Saturated fat: 1g; Cholesterol: 70mg; Sodium: 577mg; Carbohydrates: 27g; Fiber: 1g; Protein: 31g

Grilled Cheese and Tomato Soup

Grilled cheese and tomato soup is a timeless combination. There's something so comforting about dunking a melty, crispy sandwich into a big bowl of hot, creamy, nourishing tomato soup. Plus, both components freeze and reheat beautifully, making them delicious meal prep recipes. Using mayonnaise is an old restaurant trick that helps give grilled cheese that beloved golden, crispy, flavorful restaurant-quality crunch on the outside, but you can use butter instead if you prefer.

NUT-FREE, VEGETARIAN

PREP TIME: 10 minutes
TOTAL COOK TIME:
42 minutes

APPROX. PRESSURE BUILD: 10 minutes
PRESSURE COOK:
15 minutes
PRESSURE RELEASE:
natural for 10 minutes,
then quick

AIR CRISP TIME: 7 minutes
at 375°F

ACCESSORIES: Deluxe
Reversible Rack

12 slices cheddar cheese

6 slices provolone cheese

12 slices sourdough bread, white bread, or your favorite bread

¾ cup mayonnaise

Nonstick cooking spray

1 tablespoon extra-virgin olive oil

1 small yellow onion, diced

2 garlic cloves, minced

3 (15-ounce) cans crushed tomatoes

1 cup low-sodium vegetable broth

2 tablespoons chopped fresh basil, divided

½ teaspoon dried oregano

½ teaspoon kosher salt

¼ teaspoon freshly ground black pepper

¼ cup half-and-half

1. Place 2 slices of cheddar cheese and 1 slice of provolone cheese between two slices of bread. Slather the outside of each sandwich with about 1 tablespoon of mayonnaise per side. Repeat until you have a total of 6 sandwiches.

2. Spray the Deluxe Reversible Rack with cooking spray. Place the rack in the lower steam position without the Deluxe Layer installed and lower the rack into the Foodi™ pot. Place 3 sandwiches on the rack. Next, install the Deluxe Layer on the rack and place the remaining sandwiches on it.

3. Select AIR CRISP, set temperature to 375ºF, and set time to 5 minutes. Select START/STOP to begin.

CONTINUED ▶

Grilled Cheese and Tomato Soup continued

continued

VARIATION TIP: Using crushed tomatoes makes this soup smooth without the need for pureeing the ingredients. If you would like the soup to be silky smooth, when the soup is done pressure cooking, puree it in the pot with a handheld immersion blender. Or, carefully ladle the soup into a blender in batches and puree until smooth.

STORAGE: Store in airtight containers in the refrigerator for up to 4 days or in the freezer for up to 2 months.

4. When cooking is complete, open the lid of the Foodi™ and lift out the rack. If the underside of each sandwich needs more time to crisp, flip the sandwiches over and return the rack to the pot. Select AIR CRISP, set the temperature to 375°F, and set the time to 2 minutes. Select START/STOP to begin.

5. When cooking is complete, open the lid and lift out the racks. Let the sandwiches cool at room temperature while you make the soup.

6. If any bits of cheese dripped onto the bottom of the pot while the sandwiches were cooking, carefully wipe them up with a paper towel.

7. Select SEAR/SAUTÉ and set the temperature to HI. Select START/STOP to begin.

8. Pour the olive oil into the pot and let it heat up. Once the oil is hot, add the onion and garlic and sauté for 1 minute, just until soft and fragrant. Select START/STOP.

9. Add the tomatoes, broth, 1 tablespoon of basil, oregano, salt, and pepper to the pot.

10. Assemble the pressure lid, making sure the pressure release valve is in the SEAL position. Select PRESSURE and set it to HI. Set the time to 15 minutes. Select START/STOP to begin.

11. When the pressure cooking is complete, allow the pressure to release naturally for 10 minutes. After 10 minutes, quick release the remaining pressure by moving the pressure release valve to the VENT position. Carefully remove the lid when the unit has finished releasing pressure.

12. Stir the half-and-half into the soup. Let the soup cool at room temperature, then portion it into individual containers, top each serving with some of the remaining basil, label the containers, and refrigerate or freeze. Place the cooled cheese sandwiches in separate containers, wrap them in aluminum foil, or seal them in separate zip-top bags; label and refrigerate or freeze.

Per serving: *Calories: 745; Total fat: 54g; Saturated fat: 20g; Cholesterol: 92mg; Sodium: 1041mg; Carbohydrates: 39g; Fiber: 6g; Protein: 28g*

Beef Ragù with Spaghetti

SERVES 6

Before my kids were born, I would make beef ragù on the stove top. It needed to simmer for hours in order to become the rich, fragrant, restaurant-quality meat sauce I love so much. Now, with the Foodi™, we can get the same quality and flavor in under 20 minutes—in one pot. Although there are many different styles of this sauce from different parts of Italy, such as ragù Bolognese, and modern adaptations of the classic ragù recipe feature different cuts of beef, such as short ribs or brisket, this recipe keeps it simple by using traditional ground beef and spaghetti noodles.

DAIRY-FREE, NUT-FREE, UNDER 30 MINUTES

PREP TIME: 10 minutes
TOTAL COOK TIME: 18 minutes

APPROX. PRESSURE BUILD: 10 minutes
PRESSURE COOK: 8 minute
PRESSURE RELEASE: quick

VARIATION TIP: If you prefer a thicker sauce, after pressure cooking, set your Foodi™ to SEAR/SAUTÉ on HI, and stir the sauce until it reaches your preferred thickness.

STORAGE: Store in airtight containers in the refrigerator for up to 4 days or in the freezer for up to 3 months.

- 1 tablespoon extra-virgin olive oil
- 1 pound 80% lean ground beef
- 2 medium carrots, chopped
- 2 celery stalks, chopped
- 1 small yellow onion, diced
- 3 garlic cloves, minced
- 1 teaspoon dried oregano
- 12 ounces spaghetti
- ½ cup red wine
- 3 cups beef broth
- ½ teaspoon kosher salt
- ¼ teaspoon freshly ground black pepper
- 1 (15-ounce) can crushed tomatoes
- 2 tablespoons tomato paste
- 2 tablespoons chopped fresh parsley
- Grated Parmesan cheese, for garnish (optional)

1. Select SEAR/SAUTÉ on your Ninja® Foodi™ and set the temperature to HI. Select START/STOP to begin. Let preheat for 5 minutes.

2. Pour the oil into the inner pot of the Foodi™. Once the oil is hot, add the ground beef and sauté for 4 to 5 minutes, stirring constantly to evenly brown the meat.

3. Stir in the carrots, celery, onion, garlic, and oregano and sauté for 3 to 4 minutes, just until the vegetables are soft and fragrant. Select START/STOP.

4. Evenly place the spaghetti on top of the meat and vegetables in a crisscross fashion (break the spaghetti in half,
if needed, to make it fit). Pour in the red wine and beef
broth, and season with salt and pepper. Pour the crushed
tomatoes and tomato paste on top, but do not stir. Gently
push down on the spaghetti to submerge as much of the
pasta as possible in the liquid.

5. Assemble the pressure lid, making sure the pressure
release valve is in the SEAL position. Select PRESSURE and
set it to HI. Set the time to 8 minutes. Select START/STOP
to begin.

6. When the pressure cooking is complete, quick release
the pressure by turning the pressure release valve to the
VENT position. Carefully remove the lid when the unit has
finished releasing pressure.

7. Let the pasta cool to room temperature, then portion it
into individual containers and refrigerate or freeze. Before
serving, garnish with the parsley and Parmesan cheese,
if using.

Per serving: *Calories: 491; Total fat: 19g; Saturated fat: 6g;*
Cholesterol: 54mg; Sodium: 753mg; Carbohydrates: 53g; Fiber: 4g;
Protein: 24g

WEEK 3: HEALTHY HITS

This is a week where we focus on the freshest whole-food ingredients to make healthy, nourishing meals. This week's recipes are full of nutrients and will still satisfy both sweet and savory cravings.

SHOPPING LIST

Check your pantry for: nonstick cooking spray, extra-virgin olive oil, chicken broth, soy sauce, light brown sugar, vanilla extract, honey, kosher salt, black pepper, curry powder, turmeric, cumin, and cinnamon.

VEGETABLES, HERBS, AND SPICES

- 2 cups broccoli florets
- 1 cup fresh packed baby spinach
- 1 small yellow onion
- 6 garlic cloves
- ½ teaspoon minced fresh ginger
- ¼ cup chopped fresh cilantro
- 1 lime
- 2 tablespoons freshly squeezed lime juice
- Salad greens
- Sliced scallions (optional)

PROTEIN

- 6 (4-ounce) skinless salmon fillets
- 1½ pounds boneless, skinless chicken thighs

GRAINS

- 2 cups rolled oats
- 2 cups long-grain rice, plus additional cooked rice
- 2 cups jasmine rice
- Naan bread

DAIRY

- 8 tablespoons (1 stick) unsalted butter

OTHER

- 1 (14.5-ounce) can chickpeas
- 1 (14.5-ounce) can diced tomatoes
- 1 tablespoon chia seeds or poppy seeds
- 1 (14.5-ounce) can full-fat coconut milk
- ½ cup sliced almonds
- Sesame seeds (optional)

MEAL PREP MENU

	BREAKFAST	LUNCH	DINNER
Day 1	Cinnamon-Almond Granola	Teriyaki Salmon, Broccoli, and Rice	Chickpea Curry served with naan bread
Day 2	Cinnamon-Almond Granola	Cilantro-Lime Chicken and Rice	Teriyaki Salmon, Broccoli, and Rice
Day 3	Cinnamon-Almond Granola	Teriyaki Salmon served over salad	Cilantro-Lime Chicken served over rice
Day 4	Cinnamon-Almond Granola	Chickpea Curry served with rice	Teriyaki Salmon served over salad
Day 5	Cinnamon-Almond Granola	Cilantro-Lime Chicken served over salad	Chickpea Curry served with rice

STEP-BY-STEP PREP

1. Fully prepare the **Cinnamon-Almond Granola** (page 49).

2. While the granola is cooking, mince the garlic and divide it according to recipe measurements for the remaining three recipes. Dice the onions for the **Chickpea Curry** (page 53) and **Cilantro-Lime Chicken and Rice** (page 51). Mince the ginger and set it aside for the **Teriyaki Salmon, Broccoli, and Rice** (page 55).

3. When the granola is done cooking, spread it on parchment paper and let it cool completely at room temperature. Once the granola is cool, break it up into pieces, then transfer it to one or two large mason jars or other airtight food containers. Label the container(s) and store them in a cool, dark place. Wash and dry the pot.

4. Fully prepare the **Cilantro-Lime Chicken and Rice**. When the recipe is finished cooking, let it cool completely at room temperature, then portion it into containers. In one of those containers, skip the rice and add salad greens off to the side. Place the additional rice in a separate container for the Chickpea Curry. Label and refrigerate.

5. Fully prepare the **Chickpea Curry**. When the recipe is done cooking, let it cool completely at room temperature, then portion it into containers, label, and refrigerate. Place one portion of curry in with the extra rice portion from the Cilantro-Lime Chicken and Rice.

6. Fully prepare the **Teriyaki Salmon, Broccoli, and Rice**. When the recipe is done cooking, let it cool completely at room temperature, then portion it into containers, label, and refrigerate. In one of those portions, skip the rice and broccoli and add a green salad to the side.

Cinnamon-Almond Granola

SERVES 6

This is one of my favorite breakfasts to make in the Foodi™—not only does it taste delicious, but it also makes the house smell amazing. Layer it in Fruit and Granola Yogurt Parfaits (page 118), or pack it up as an afternoon snack.

VEGETARIAN

PREP TIME: 5 minutes, plus 10 minutes to cool
TOTAL COOK TIME: 25 minutes

AIR CRISP: 15 minutes at 300°F

VARIATION TIP: After you've made this base recipe, try mixing in other flavorful ingredients before crisping, such as dehydrated berries, different nuts, or flaxseeds. Or, mix in mini chocolate chips or butterscotch chips after it's done crisping, once it's fully cooled.

STORAGE: Keep granola in an airtight container at room temperature for up to 1 month.

8 tablespoons (1 stick) unsalted butter

¼ cup packed light brown sugar

¼ cup honey

2 teaspoons vanilla extract

2 cups rolled oats

½ cup sliced almonds

1 tablespoon chia seeds or poppy seeds

½ teaspoon cinnamon

1. Line a baking sheet with parchment paper. Set aside.

2. Select SEAR/SAUTÉ on your Ninja® Foodi™ and set the temperature to HI. Select START/STOP to begin.

3. Add the butter to the pot. Once the butter is melted, stir in the brown sugar, honey, and vanilla until the sugar is dissolved. Mix in the oats, almonds, chia seeds, and cinnamon.

4. Close the crisping lid, select AIR CRISP, set the temperature to 300°F, and set the timer to 15 minutes. Select START/STOP to begin.

5. After 5 minutes, open the lid and stir the granola. Close the lid and cook for 5 additional minutes. Repeat after another 5 minutes, until the granola has cooked for 15 minutes total. The granola is done when it's evenly browned.

6. When cooking is complete, spread the granola on the prepared baking sheet. Let the granola cool for 10 minutes, then break it up; transfer to airtight containers.

Per serving: Calories: 416; Total fat: 22g; Saturated fat: 11g; Cholesterol: 41mg; Sodium: 10mg; Carbohydrates: 48g; Fiber: 6g; Protein: 8g

Cilantro-Lime Chicken and Rice

SERVES 6

It's always good to have at least one chicken and rice dish in your pocket. This one is packed with flavor and has a bright cilantro-lime twist. Cooking the chicken on the Deluxe Reversible Rack above the rice allows all of those great flavors to seep into the rice without weighing it dough.

DAIRY-FREE, GLUTEN-FREE, NUT-FREE

PREP TIME: 10 minutes
TOTAL COOK TIME: 27 minutes

APPROX. PRESSURE BUILD: 10 minutes
PRESSURE COOK: 7 minutes
PRESSURE RELEASE: natural for 5 minutes, then quick

ACCESSORIES: Deluxe Reversible Rack

PREP TIP: If you'd like even more flavor and have more time, marinate the chicken in the olive oil, spices, onion, and garlic in a gallon-size resealable bag for 30 minutes. Then, continue with step 2 of the directions, sautéing the contents of the bag all together.

2 tablespoons extra-virgin olive oil

1½ pounds boneless, *double* skinless chicken thighs

½ teaspoon kosher salt

¼ teaspoon freshly ground black pepper

½ teaspoon ground cumin

¼ teaspoon curry powder

½ small yellow onion, diced

2 garlic cloves, minced

2 cups long-grain rice

2½ cups chicken broth

2 tablespoons freshly squeezed lime juice

4 tablespoons chopped fresh cilantro, divided

Nonstick cooking spray

Salad greens, for serving

1 lime, cut into wedges

1. Select SEAR/SAUTÉ on your Ninja® Foodi™ and set the temperature to HI. Select START/STOP to begin. Let preheat for 5 minutes.

2. Pour the olive oil into the Foodi™ pot. Once the oil is hot, add the chicken, salt, pepper, cumin, and curry powder and cook the chicken for 5 to 6 minutes per side, just until it is browned on all sides. Transfer the chicken to a plate and set aside.

3. Add the onion and garlic and sauté for 2 to 3 minutes, just until soft and fragrant. As you are sautéing, use a wooden spoon to scrape up any browned bits at the bottom of the pan. Select START/STOP.

4. Place the rice in the pot in an even layer, then pour in the broth, lime juice, and 2 tablespoons of cilantro. Stir to combine.

CONTINUED ▶

Cilantro-Lime Chicken and Rice continued

STORAGE: Store in airtight containers in the refrigerator for up to 4 days or in the freezer for up to 2 months.

5. Spray the reversible racks with cooking spray. Place the Deluxe Reversible Rack in the higher broil position without the Deluxe Layer installed and lower it into the Foodi™ pot over the rice. Place the chicken on the rack.

6. Assemble the pressure lid, making sure the pressure release valve is in the SEAL position. Select PRESSURE and set it to HI. Set the time to 7 minutes. Select START/STOP to begin.

7. When the pressure cooking is complete, allow the pressure to release naturally for 10 minutes. After 10 minutes, quick release the remaining pressure by moving the pressure release valve to the VENT position. Carefully remove the lid when the unit has finished releasing pressure.

8. Lift out the rack with the chicken. Let the chicken cool to room temperature, then portion the chicken and rice into individual containers. In one of those containers, skip the rice and add salad greens off to the side. Garnish each portion with the remaining 2 tablespoons of cilantro and a lime wedge, then label and refrigerate or freeze. (If freezing, store the greens separately and add after thawing.)

Per serving: Calories: 418; Total fat: 10g; Saturated fat: 2g; Cholesterol: 109mg; Sodium: 595mg; Carbohydrates: 52g; Fiber: 1g; Protein: 28g

Chickpea Curry

Curry is not only one of the world's most popular dishes but also possibly one of the oldest. People have been eating curry for more than 4,500 years. The base usually consists of garlic, ginger, and turmeric; from there, dozens of different types of aromatic, flavorful curries exist. This chickpea curry is a vegan, Indian-inspired recipe that's become one of my favorite nourishing meals. It's delightful served with naan, rice, couscous, or quinoa.

DAIRY-FREE, NUT-FREE, VEGAN

PREP TIME: 10 minutes
TOTAL COOK TIME: 23 minutes

APPROX. PRESSURE BUILD: 10 minutes
PRESSURE COOK: 4 minutes
PRESSURE RELEASE: quick

SAUTÉ: 4 minutes + 5 minutes

STORAGE: Store in airtight containers in the refrigerator for up to 4 days or in the freezer for up to 2 months.

- 2 tablespoons extra-virgin olive oil
- ½ small yellow onion, diced
- 3 garlic cloves, minced
- 1 (14.5-ounce) can chickpeas, drained and rinsed
- ½ tablespoon curry powder
- 1 teaspoon ground turmeric
- ½ teaspoon ground cumin
- ½ teaspoon kosher salt
- ¼ teaspoon freshly ground black pepper
- 1 (14.5-ounce) can full-fat coconut milk
- 1 (14.5-ounce) can diced tomatoes, drained
- 1 cup fresh baby spinach
- Cooked rice and naan, for serving

1. Select SEAR/SAUTÉ on your Ninja® Foodi™ and set the temperature to HI. Select START/STOP to begin. Let preheat for 5 minutes.

2. Pour the olive oil into the pot. Once the oil is hot, add the onion and garlic and sauté for 2 minutes, just until they are soft and fragrant.

3. Add the chickpeas, curry powder, turmeric, cumin, salt, pepper, and coconut milk. Stir to combine. Select START/STOP.

4. Pour the tomatoes on top and gently push down to submerge them in the liquid.

CONTINUED ▶

5. Assemble the pressure lid, making sure the pressure release valve is in the SEAL position. Select PRESSURE and set it to HI. Set the time to 4 minutes. Select START/STOP to begin.

6. When the pressure cooking is complete, quick release the pressure by turning the pressure release valve to the VENT position. Carefully remove the lid when the unit has finished releasing pressure.

7. Select SEAR/SAUTÉ and set the temperature to MD. Select START/STOP to begin.

8. Stir in the spinach and cook until the sauce has thickened and the spinach has wilted, about 5 minutes.

9. Let the curry cool to room temperature, then portion it into individual containers for the week. Add rice to two of the containers for lunch on day 4 and dinner on day 5. Label and refrigerate or freeze the containers. Place the naan bread in a resealable bag to serve with dinner on day 1.

Per serving: Calories: 430; Total fat: 23g; Saturated fat: 15g; Cholesterol: 0mg; Sodium: 440mg; Carbohydrates: 49g; Fiber: 6g; Protein: 10g

Teriyaki Salmon, Broccoli, and Rice

SERVES 6

Salmon is a hearty, delicious pink fish packed with omega-3 fatty acids—which are said to help with brain function and heart health—as well as potassium, selenium, and vitamin B$_{12}$. In this recipe, the salmon cooks at the same time as the rice and broccoli, making dinnertime and cleanup a snap. A sweet, tangy teriyaki glaze brings the whole dish together. Try this recipe with different vegetables, like carrots, snap peas, or bok choy.

DAIRY-FREE, NUT-FREE, ONE AND DONE, UNDER 30 MINUTES

PREP TIME: 5 minutes
TOTAL COOK TIME: 19 minutes

APPROX. PRESSURE BUILD: 10 minutes
PRESSURE COOK: 2 minutes
PRESSURE RELEASE: natural for 5 minutes, then quick

BROIL: 7 minutes

ACCESSORIES: Deluxe Reversible Rack

STORAGE: Refrigerate in airtight containers for up to 3 or 4 days. This salmon dish is best enjoyed earlier in your meal planning week.

Nonstick cooking spray

2 cups water

2 cups jasmine rice, rinsed

6 (4-ounce) skinless salmon fillets

½ teaspoon kosher salt

¼ teaspoon freshly ground black pepper

½ cup soy sauce

1 teaspoon honey

¼ cup brown sugar

½ teaspoon minced fresh ginger

1 garlic clove, minced

2 cups broccoli florets

Sliced scallions and sesame seeds for serving (optional)

1. Spray the Deluxe Reversible Rack with cooking spray.

2. Combine the water and rice in the pot and stir to combine. Place the Deluxe Reversible Rack in the lower steam position without the Deluxe Layer installed and lower the rack into the pot of your Ninja® Foodi™.

3. Season the salmon with salt and pepper, then place it on the rack.

4. Assemble the pressure lid, making sure the pressure release valve is in the SEAL position. Select PRESSURE and set it to HI. Set the time to 2 minutes. Select START/STOP to begin.

CONTINUED ▶

5. Meanwhile, in a medium bowl, stir together the soy sauce, honey, brown sugar, ginger, and garlic until the sugar is dissolved. Place half of the teriyaki mixture in a separate large bowl. Add the broccoli florets and toss well; set aside.

6. When the pressure cooking is complete, quick release the pressure by turning the pressure release valve to the VENT position. Carefully remove the lid when the unit has finished releasing pressure.

7. Gently pat the salmon dry with a paper towel. Brush the remaining teriyaki glaze evenly on top of the fish. Install the Deluxe Layer on the rack and place the broccoli on it.

8. Close the crisping lid. Select BROIL and set the time to 7 minutes. Select START/STOP to begin. After 5 minutes, check for doneness: the salmon will turn an opaque, deeper-colored pink-orange and should flake easily when poked with a fork, and the broccoli will be fork-tender.

9. When cooking is complete, remove the salmon and broccoli from the rack and let them cool completely at room temperature. Portion out the salmon, broccoli, and rice into containers. In one of the containers, skip the broccoli and rice and add salad greens off to the side for dinner on day 4. Garnish each portion with sliced scallions and sesame seeds (if using), then label and refrigerate.

Per serving: Calories: 499; Total fat: 12g; Saturated fat: 4g; Cholesterol: 57mg; Sodium: 928mg; Carbohydrates: 65g; Fiber: 2g; Protein: 30g

WEEK 4: PEPPER POWER

Bell peppers are inexpensive, versatile vegetables that impart so much flavor for breakfast, lunch, and dinner. They're an excellent source of vitamin A, vitamin C, and potassium. You can use red, green, orange, or yellow bell peppers interchangeably in all these recipes.

SHOPPING LIST

Check your pantry for: extra-virgin olive oil, beef broth, chicken broth, kosher salt, black pepper, dried oregano, and paprika.

VEGETABLES, HERBS, AND SPICES

- 2½ red bell peppers
- ½ cup broccoli florets
- 2 cups fresh baby spinach leaves
- 2 small yellow onions
- 3 garlic cloves
- 1 tablespoon chopped fresh parsley
- Salad greens

PROTEIN

- 6 large eggs
- 1 pound sirloin steak
- 1 pound large shrimp
- 6 ounces andouille sausage

GRAINS

- 1½ cups quick-cooking grits
- 6 hoagie rolls

DAIRY

- ¼ cup heavy (whipping) cream
- 4 tablespoons unsalted butter
- 1 cup milk (2%, 1%, or skim)
- 1½ cups shredded cheddar cheese
- 12 slices provolone cheese

OTHER

- 1 refrigerated piecrust
- 1 cup dry white wine

MEAL PREP MENU

	BREAKFAST	LUNCH	DINNER
Day 1	Loaded Vegetable Quiche	Shrimp and Grits	Cheesesteak
Day 2	Loaded Vegetable Quiche	Cheesesteak	Shrimp and Grits
Day 3	Loaded Vegetable Quiche	Shrimp and Grits	Cheesesteak
Day 4	Shrimp and Grits	Cheesesteak	Loaded Vegetable Quiche
Day 5	Loaded Vegetable Quiche	Shrimp and Grits	Cheesesteak served over salad

STEP-BY-STEP PREP

1. Dice the bell peppers and divide them according to recipe measurements for the three recipes. Dice the onions and divide them to use in the **Loaded Vegetable Quiche** (page 60) and **Cheesesteaks** (page 63). Mince the garlic and divide it to use in the **Loaded Vegetable Quiche** and **Shrimp and Grits** (page 65).

2. Fully prepare the **Loaded Vegetable Quiche**.

3. While the quiche is baking, slice the steak and measure out the ingredients for the **Cheesesteaks**. Dice the andouille sausage, and measure out the ingredients for the **Shrimp and Grits**.

4. When the quiche is done cooking, let it cool at room temperature, then place it in an airtight container, label, and refrigerate. Wash and dry the pot.

5. Fully prepare the **Cheesesteaks**. When the meat is done cooking, portion it into airtight containers, label, and refrigerate. Do not place the fillings in hoagie rolls until you are ready to eat the sandwiches, since the filling will make the bread soggy during refrigeration. Wash and dry the pot.

6. Fully prepare the **Shrimp and Grits**. When the recipe is done cooking, let it cool at room temperature, then portion it into containers, placing the grits on one side and the shrimp on the other side of each container. Label and refrigerate. Wash and dry the pot.

Loaded Vegetable Quiche

A quiche is a delicious way to sneak in lots of healthy vegetables. Typically served for breakfast or brunch, this quiche is hearty enough to enjoy for lunch or dinner. You'll want to use a Foodi™ all-purpose pan, which fits onto the Deluxe Reversible Rack. A springform pan also works great because it makes it easy to transfer the quiche to a plate.

NUT-FREE, VEGETARIAN

PREP TIME: 10 minutes
TOTAL COOK TIME:
26 minutes

BAKE/ROAST: 6 minutes at 400°F + 20 minutes at 360°F

ACCESSORIES: Deluxe Reversible Rack, Foodi™ all-purpose pan

- 6 large eggs
- ¼ cup heavy (whipping) cream
- 1 teaspoon kosher salt
- ½ teaspoon freshly ground black pepper
- 1 tablespoon extra-virgin olive oil
- 1 small onion, diced
- ½ red bell pepper, diced
- ½ cup chopped broccoli
- 1 garlic clove, minced
- 2 cups fresh baby spinach leaves
- ½ cup shredded cheddar cheese
- 1 tablespoon unsalted butter, for greasing
- 1 refrigerated piecrust

1. Select SEAR/SAUTÉ on your Ninja® Foodi™ and set the temperature to HI. Select START/STOP to begin. Let preheat for 5 minutes.

2. In a large bowl, whisk together the eggs, cream, salt, and black pepper. Set aside.

3. Pour the olive oil into the pot. Once the oil is hot, add the onion, bell pepper, broccoli, and garlic and sauté for 3 minutes. Mix in the spinach and sauté for 1 more minute, just until the spinach wilts. Select START/STOP.

4. Carefully lift the pot up and pour the vegetables into the bowl containing the egg mixture. Stir in the cheese. Cover with aluminum foil and set aside. Wipe out the pot with a paper towel and return it to the unit.

5. Lightly grease the all-purpose pan with the butter. Gently press the piecrust into the bottom and up the sides of the pan. Place the Deluxe Reversible Rack in the lower steam position without the Deluxe Layer installed and lower it into the pot. Place the all-purpose pan on the rack.

6. Close the crisping lid. Select BAKE/ROAST, set the temperature to 400°F, and set the time to 6 minutes. Select START/STOP to begin.

7. When cooking is complete, open the lid and carefully lift out the rack.

8. Pour the vegetable-egg mixture into the crust, then lower the rack back into the pot. Close the crisping lid. Select BAKE/ROAST, set the temperature to 360°F, and set the time to 20 minutes. Select START/STOP to begin.

9. When cooking is complete, open the lid, remove the foil, and test for doneness. If a toothpick inserted into the center of the quiche comes out clean, it's fully cooked. If it's not ready, cook the quiche for 2 to 4 minutes longer.

10. Let the quiche cool to room temperature, then portion slices into individual containers, label, and refrigerate or freeze.

Per serving: Calories: 363; Total fat: 26g; Saturated fat: 11g; Cholesterol: 214mg; Sodium: 511mg; Carbohydrates: 23g; Fiber: 1g; Protein: 11g

VARIATION TIP: This quiche recipe is versatile and forgiving, allowing you to add most hearty vegetables to the mix. Try green peppers, mushrooms, or asparagus; just be sure to cut the vegetables to about the same size so they cook evenly. You can also make it vegan by substituting dairy-free cheese and almond milk for the cheddar cheese and heavy cream.

STORAGE: Store in airtight containers in the refrigerator for up to 4 days or in the freezer for up to 3 months.

Cheesesteaks

I still vividly remember the first time I had an authentic Philly cheesesteak at Pat's King of Steaks, where founder Pat Olivieri invented the cheesesteak in 1930. The paper-thin slices of steak with melty cheese and aromatic onions was like no steak sandwich I had ever had before. This recipe is inspired by the original, and it's best served with a heaping pile of salty, crunchy potato chips.

NUT-FREE

PREP TIME: 10 minutes
TOTAL COOK TIME:
30 minutes

APPROX. PRESSURE BUILD: 10 minutes
PRESSURE COOK:
8 minutes
PRESSURE RELEASE:
natural for 10 minutes, then quick

SAUTÉ: 2 minutes

PREP TIP: Slicing the steak while it's partially frozen makes it easier to make thin slices. You can also cook the meat directly in the pot from frozen.

STORAGE: Store in airtight containers in the refrigerator for up to 4 days or in the freezer for up to 2 months.

2 tablespoons extra-virgin olive oil

1 red bell pepper, sliced

1 small yellow onion, sliced

½ teaspoon dried oregano

1 teaspoon kosher salt

¼ teaspoon freshly ground black pepper

1 pound sirloin steak, thinly sliced

1½ cups beef broth

12 slices provolone cheese

6 hoagie rolls, for serving

Salad greens, for serving

1. Select SEAR/SAUTÉ on your Ninja® Foodi™ and set the temperature to HI. Select START/STOP to begin. Let preheat for 5 minutes.

2. Pour the olive oil into the pot. Once the oil is hot, add the red bell pepper, onion, oregano, salt, and black pepper and sauté for about 2 minutes. Select START/STOP.

3. Place the steak strips on top of the vegetables, then pour the beef broth into the pot.

4. Assemble the pressure lid, making sure the pressure release valve is in the SEAL position. Select PRESSURE and set it to HI. Set the time to 8 minutes. Select START/STOP to begin.

CONTINUED ▶

5. When the pressure cooking is complete, allow the pressure to release naturally for 10 minutes. After 10 minutes, quick release the remaining pressure by moving the pressure release valve to the VENT position. Carefully remove the lid when the unit has finished releasing pressure.

6. Add the cheese to the pot and let it melt slightly, 1 to 2 minutes.

7. Let the steak cool to room temperature, then portion it into individual airtight containers, label, and refrigerate or freeze. Do not place the filling on the hoagie rolls, or the bread will become soggy in the refrigerator.

8. When ready to eat, reheat and scoop portions into hoagie rolls. For dinner on day 5, serve the steak over salad greens.

Per serving: Calories: 515; Total fat: 30g; Saturated fat: 14g; Cholesterol: 93mg; Sodium: 836mg; Carbohydrates: 25g; Fiber: 2g; Protein: 35g

Shrimp and Grits

Shrimp and grits may have begun as a breakfast dish in South Carolina, but it's now a beloved lunch and dinner dish as well on tables across the country. In this recipe, creamy grits begin pressure cooking in a savory gravy in the Foodi™, and then well-seasoned shrimp are added to cook during the final minutes. To keep the grits from sticking to the pot, stir constantly while sautéing, and scrape up any browned bits at the bottom of the pot before you pressure cook.

NUT-FREE

PREP TIME: 5 minutes
TOTAL COOK TIME:
26 minutes

APPROX. PRESSURE
BUILD: 10 minutes
PRESSURE COOK:
0 minutes
PRESSURE RELEASE:
quick

BAKE/ROAST: 10 minutes
at 375°F

SAUTÉ: 6 minutes

ACCESSORIES: Deluxe
Reversible Rack

3 tablespoons
   unsalted butter

6 ounces andouille
   sausage, diced

1 red bell pepper, diced

2 garlic cloves, minced

1½ cups quick-cooking
   grits

1 teaspoon kosher salt

¼ teaspoon freshly
   ground black pepper

1 cup dry white wine

2 (14.5-ounce) cans
   chicken broth

1 pound large shrimp,
   peeled and deveined

2 tablespoons
   extra-virgin olive oil

½ teaspoon dried oregano

½ teaspoon paprika

1 cup milk

1 cup shredded
   cheddar cheese

1 tablespoon chopped fresh
   parsley, for serving

1. Select SEAR/SAUTÉ on your Ninja® Foodi™ and set the temperature to HI. Select START/STOP to begin. Let preheat for 5 minutes.

2. Place the butter in the pot. Once the butter has melted, add the sausage and sauté for 2 to 3 minutes, until cooked. Stir in the red bell pepper, garlic, grits, salt, and pepper and sauté, stirring constantly, for 2 to 3 minutes, just until the vegetables become soft and fragrant. Select START/STOP.

3. Pour in the wine and the broth, using a wooden spoon to scrape up any browned bits from the bottom of the pot.

CONTINUED ▶

Shrimp and Grits continued

STORAGE: Store the shrimp and grits together in airtight containers in the refrigerator for up to 4 days, or freeze the grits and shrimp in separate airtight containers for up to 2 months. To reheat in the Foodi™, select SEAR/SAUTÉ, set the temperature to HI, and select START/STOP to begin. Place leftover grits and shrimp in the pot along with 1 tablespoon of water or milk. Stir until reheated, 2 to 3 minutes. To reheat in the microwave, place a serving in a microwave-safe bowl, stir in 1 tablespoon of water or milk, and reheat in 30-second increments.

4. Assemble the pressure lid, making sure the pressure release valve is in the SEAL position. Select PRESSURE and set it to HI. Set the time to 0 minutes. Select START/STOP to begin.

5. Meanwhile, in a large bowl, toss together the shrimp, olive oil, oregano, and paprika.

6. When the pressure cooking is complete, quick release the pressure by turning the pressure release valve to the VENT position. Carefully remove the lid when the unit has finished releasing pressure.

7. Stir in the milk. Place the Deluxe Reversible Rack in the higher broil position, then lower the rack into the pot. Place the seasoned shrimp on the rack.

8. Close the crisping lid. Select BAKE/ROAST, set the temperature to 375ºF, and set the time to 5 minutes. Select START/STOP to begin.

9. When cooking is complete, open the crisping lid and remove the rack. Immediately stir the cheese into the grits until well combined.

10. Let the shrimp and grits cool to room temperature, then portion them into individual containers, placing the grits on one side of each container and the shrimp on the other side. Label and refrigerate or freeze. When ready to eat, reheat and sprinkle with the parsley.

Per serving: Calories: 446; Total fat: 27g; Saturated fat: 11g; Cholesterol: 153mg; Sodium: 1032mg; Carbohydrates: 20g; Fiber: 1g; Protein: 25g

WEEK 5: CITRUS STARS

Citrus adds a vibrant, bright, light flavor to so many dishes, both sweet and savory. This week's menu celebrates lemon and lime flavors in flavorful recipes you can easily create in one day.

SHOPPING LIST

Check your pantry for: extra-virgin olive oil, chicken broth, vegetable broth, all-purpose flour, baking powder, baking soda, sugar, vegetable oil, vanilla extract, chili powder, paprika, ground cumin, garlic powder, onion powder, kosher salt, and black pepper.

FRUIT, VEGETABLES, HERBS, AND SPICES

- 3 carrots
- 2 celery stalks
- 2 small onions
- 6 garlic cloves
- 1 cup shredded lettuce
- 1 cup baby spinach
- 1 cup frozen peas
- 2 or 3 radishes
- 1 tablespoon minced fresh ginger
- 1 lemon
- ½ cup plus 2 tablespoons freshly squeezed lemon juice
- 1 teaspoon grated lemon zest
- 1 tablespoon freshly squeezed lime juice
- ½ cup blueberries
- 1 avocado
- 2 tablespoons chopped fresh basil
- 1 tablespoon chopped fresh dill
- 1 tablespoon chopped fresh cilantro
- Salad greens

PROTEIN

- 2 large eggs
- 1½ pounds boneless, skinless chicken thighs
- 24 large shrimp

GRAINS AND NOODLES

- 2 cups white rice
- 1 cup orzo
- 6 (10-inch) flour tortillas

DAIRY

- 1 tablespoon sour cream
- 3 tablespoons unsalted butter
- Sour cream (optional)

OTHER

- 2 (14.5-ounce) cans chickpeas
- 1 tablespoon tequila
- Guacamole (optional)
- Pico de gallo (optional)

MEAL PREP MENU

	BREAKFAST	LUNCH	DINNER
Day 1	Lemon-Blueberry Mini Muffins	Lemon, Chickpea, and Orzo Soup	Tequila, Lime, and Chipotle Shrimp Tacos
Day 2	Lemon-Blueberry Mini Muffins	Tequila, Lime, and Chipotle Shrimp Tacos	Lemon-Garlic Chicken and Rice
Day 3	Lemon-Blueberry Mini Muffins	Lemon, Chickpea, and Orzo Soup	Tequila, Lime, and Chipotle Shrimp Tacos
Day 4	Lemon-Blueberry Mini Muffins	Tequila, Lime, and Chipotle Shrimp served over salad	Lemon-Garlic Chicken served over salad
Day 5	Lemon-Blueberry Mini Muffins	Lemon, Chickpea, and Orzo Soup	Lemon-Garlic Chicken and Rice

STEP-BY-STEP PREP

1. Zest the lemons for the **Lemon-Blueberry Mini Muffins** (page 70). Juice the lemons and divide it according to the measurements for the **Lemon-Blueberry Mini Muffins**, **Lemon-Garlic Chicken and Rice** (page 72), and **Lemon, Chickpea, and Orzo Soup** (page 74).

2. Fully prepare the **Lemon-Blueberry Mini Muffins**.

3. While the muffins are baking, dice the onions and mince the garlic and ginger for the **Lemon-Garlic Chicken and Rice** and **Lemon, Chickpea, and Orzo Soup**; divide into separate bowls according to the measurements in the remaining recipes.

4. When the muffins are done, let them cool, then transfer them to an airtight container. Wash and dry the pot.

5. Fully prepare the **Lemon-Garlic Chicken and Rice**. While the chicken is pressure cooking, chop the carrots and celery for the **Lemon, Chickpea, and Orzo Soup**.

6. When the **Lemon-Garlic Chicken and Rice** is done cooking, portion it into containers. Wash the pot and wipe it dry.

7. Fully prepare the **Lemon, Chickpea, and Orzo Soup**.

8. While the soup is cooking, mix together the spice marinade (olive oil through black pepper) for the **Tequila, Lime, and Chipotle Shrimp Tacos** (page 77) in a gallon-size resealable bag. Set aside.

9. After you quick release the pressure for the soup, add the shrimp to the resealable bag and marinate for 5 minutes.

10. When the soup is done cooking, ladle portions into airtight containers, leaving at least 1 inch of space at the top. Let the soup cool to room temperature, then label and refrigerate or freeze.

11. Prepare the **Tequila, Lime, and Chipotle Shrimp Tacos** from step 2 through step 4. When the shrimp is done cooking, place it in a large airtight container, label, and refrigerate or freeze. Wash the pot and wipe it dry.

Lemon-Blueberry Mini Muffins

Skip a trip to the bakery, and enjoy your own homemade mini muffins. These are packable, portable, meal-plan-friendly bites that are enjoyable any time of day—not just for breakfast. These mini muffins can be made in two Foodi™ mini molds—one on each rack of the Deluxe Reversible Rack—or in two batches if you only have one mold. No mini molds? No problem: You can also make these in individual silicone muffin molds placed inside a baking pan. The cook time is the same.

NUT-FREE, VEGETARIAN

PREP TIME: 10 minutes
TOTAL COOK TIME:
35 minutes

APPROX. PRESSURE BUILD: 10 minutes
PRESSURE COOK:
15 minutes
PRESSURE RELEASE:
natural for 5 minutes, then quick

AIR CRISP: 5 minutes at 350°F

ACCESSORIES: Deluxe Reversible Rack, Foodi™ mini molds

1¼ **cup all-purpose flour**

1 **teaspoon baking powder**

½ **teaspoon baking soda**

¼ **teaspoon kosher salt**

½ **cup granulated sugar**

¼ **cup vegetable oil**

1 **tablespoon sour cream**

1 **teaspoon vanilla extract**

1 **tablespoon freshly squeezed lemon juice**

1 **teaspoon grated lemon zest**

2 **large eggs**

½ **cup blueberries**

1 **cup water**

1. In a large bowl, whisk together the flour, baking powder, baking soda, and salt.

2. In a stand mixer or a separate large bowl, mix together the sugar, vegetable oil, sour cream, vanilla, lemon juice, and lemon zest. Beat in the eggs one at a time until incorporated.

3. Beat the dry ingredients into the wet ingredients, then gently fold in the blueberries.

4. Scoop the batter into the Foodi™ mini mold cups, filling each cup three-quarters full. Cover each mold tightly with aluminum foil.

5. Pour the water into the pot. Place the Deluxe Reversible Rack in the lower steam position without the Deluxe Layer installed and lower the rack into the Ninja® Foodi™ pot. Place one of the filled molds on the rack. Next, install the Deluxe Layer on the rack and place the remaining filled mold on it.

6. Assemble the pressure lid, making sure the pressure release valve is in the SEAL position. Select PRESSURE and set it to HI. Set the time to 15 minutes. Select START/STOP to begin.

7. When the pressure cooking is complete, allow the pressure to release naturally for 5 minutes. After 5 minutes, quick release the remaining pressure by moving the pressure release valve to the VENT position. Carefully remove the lid when the unit has finished releasing pressure.

8. Lift the rack with the molds out of the pot. Remove the foil from the top of each mold. Pour out any liquid that has accumulated in the bottom of the pot, then return the pot to the Foodi™ unit. Carefully lower the rack with molds into the pot.

9. Close the crisping lid. Select AIR CRISP, set the temperature to 350°F, and set the time to 5 minutes. Select START/STOP to begin.

10. When the cooking is complete, remove the rack from the Foodi™. Let the muffins cool to room temperature, then portion them into individual containers, label, and refrigerate or freeze.

PREP TIP: Since these are mini muffins, it's best to use the smallest blueberries in this recipe.

STORAGE: Store in airtight containers in the refrigerator for up to 4 days or in the freezer for up to 3 months.

Per serving (1 muffin): *Calories: 139; Total fat: 6g; Saturated fat: 1g; Cholesterol: 32mg; Sodium: 91mg; Carbohydrates: 20g; Fiber: 1g; Protein: 2g*

Lemon-Garlic Chicken and Rice

SERVES 6

Variations of lemon chicken can be found in many different cultures, but my favorite is a mouthwatering dish of grilled chicken thighs seasoned liberally with lemon, garlic, and herbs that I devoured in Greece. It was served on a bed of roasted potatoes. So simple, yet the lemon flavors shined. This recipe is inspired by that Greek dish, but with some ginger for zing and fresh basil for a hit of freshness.

NUT-FREE

PREP TIME: 5 minutes
TOTAL COOK TIME:
30 minutes

APPROX. PRESSURE
BUILD: 10 minutes
PRESSURE COOK:
8 minutes
PRESSURE RELEASE:
natural for 5 minutes, then
quick

SAUTÉ: 7 minutes

ACCESSORIES: Deluxe
Reversible Rack

VARIATION TIP: This
versatile chicken dish
is delicious served over
rice, noodles, couscous,
quinoa, or salad.

1½ pounds boneless,
skinless chicken thighs

½ teaspoon kosher salt

¼ teaspoon freshly
ground black pepper

3 tablespoons
extra-virgin olive oil

1 tablespoon freshly
squeezed lemon juice

3 tablespoons
unsalted butter

1 small yellow onion, diced

2 garlic cloves, minced

1 tablespoon minced
fresh ginger

2 tablespoons chopped
fresh basil

2 cups chicken
broth or water

2 cups white rice

Salad greens, for serving

1. Select SEAR/SAUTÉ on your Ninja® Foodi™ and set the temperature to HI. Select START/STOP to begin. Let preheat for 5 minutes.

2. Meanwhile, season the chicken with the salt and pepper.

3. Pour the olive oil into the pot. Once the oil is hot, add the chicken and sauté for 4 to 5 minutes, browning it on both sides. Add the lemon juice and butter to the pot, then stir in the onion, garlic, ginger, and basil. Sauté for about 2 minutes, then select START/STOP. Leaving the vegetables in the pot, transfer the chicken to a plate or bowl and set aside.

4. Pour the broth into the pot. Using a wooden spoon, gently scrape up any browned bits at the bottom of the pot.

5. Pour the rice into the pot and stir to submerge the rice in the liquid.

6. Place the Deluxe Reversible Rack in the higher broil position, then lower it into the pot over the rice and liquid. Place the chicken on the rack.

7. Assemble the pressure lid, making sure the pressure release valve is in the SEAL position. Select PRESSURE and set it to HI. Set the time to 8 minutes. Select START/STOP to begin.

8. When the pressure cooking is complete, allow the pressure to release naturally for 5 minutes. After 5 minutes, quick release the remaining pressure by moving the pressure release valve to the VENT position. Carefully remove the lid when the unit has finished releasing pressure.

9. Let the chicken and rice cool to room temperature, then portion them into individual containers for the week. In one container, add salad greens instead of rice. Label the containers and refrigerate or freeze. (If freezing, store the greens separately.)

STORAGE: Store in airtight containers in the refrigerator for up to 4 days or in the freezer for up to 3 months.

Per serving: Calories: 492; Total fat: 18g; Saturated fat: 6g; Cholesterol: 122mg; Sodium: 208mg; Carbohydrates: 54g; Fiber: 1g; Protein: 27g

Lemon, Chickpea, and Orzo Soup

This is a soul-soothing soup that will warm you up on the chilliest of days. It's a delicious vegan alternative to traditional chicken noodle soup. Because the orzo soaks up the liquid, it's best to enjoy this soup earlier in your meal planning week. For meal prep, you can reheat single servings with a cup of stock or water and a squeeze of fresh lemon juice.

DAIRY-FREE, NUT-FREE, UNDER 30 MINUTES, VEGAN

PREP TIME: 10 minutes
TOTAL COOK TIME: 20 minutes

APPROX. PRESSURE BUILD: 10 minutes
PRESSURE COOK: 5 minutes
PRESSURE RELEASE: quick

SAUTÉ: 3 minutes

STORAGE: Store the soup in airtight containers in the refrigerator for up to 4 days or in the freezer for up to 2 months. If freezing, it's best to cook the soup without the orzo, then cook the orzo when reheating the soup.

2 tablespoons extra-virgin olive oil

3 carrots, chopped

2 celery stalks, chopped

1 small yellow onion, diced

4 garlic cloves, minced

2 (14.5-ounce) cans chickpeas, drained and rinsed

1 cup orzo

3 (14.5-ounce) cans vegetable stock (6 cups)

½ cup freshly squeezed lemon juice

½ teaspoon kosher salt

¼ teaspoon freshly ground black pepper

1 tablespoon chopped fresh dill

1 packed cup fresh baby spinach

1 cup frozen peas

1 lemon, cut into wedges

1. Select SEAR/SAUTÉ on your Ninja® Foodi™ and set the temperature to HI. Select START/STOP to begin. Let preheat for 5 minutes.

2. Pour the olive oil into the pot. Once the oil is hot, add the carrots and sauté for 1 minute. Stir in the celery, onion, and garlic and sauté for 2 minutes, just until the vegetables are soft and fragrant. Select START/STOP.

3. Pour in the chickpeas, then spread the orzo in an even layer on top. Pour in the vegetable stock and lemon juice, and season with the salt and pepper.

4. Assemble pressure lid, making sure the pressure release valve is in the SEAL position. Select PRESSURE and set it to HI. Set the time to 5 minutes. Select START/STOP to begin.

5. When the pressure cooking is complete, quick release the pressure by turning the pressure release valve to the VENT position. Carefully remove the lid when the unit has finished releasing pressure.

6. Immediately stir in the dill, spinach, and frozen peas, and cook for 1 to 2 minutes, just until the peas have thawed and the spinach is wilted.

7. Let the dish cool to room temperature, then portion it into individual containers for the week with a lemon wedge for each portion. Label the containers and refrigerate or freeze.

Per serving: *Calories: 232; Total fat: 5g; Saturated fat: 1g; Cholesterol: 0mg; Sodium: 824mg; Carbohydrates: 42g; Fiber: 6g; Protein: 7g*

Tequila, Lime, and Chipotle Shrimp Tacos

SERVES 6

This is my absolute favorite way to make shrimp in the Foodi™. It's so easy and fast, and each bite bursts with flavor. If you have a premixed chipotle seasoning, you can use that instead of the individual spices. The tequila adds a nice layer of flavor to the shrimp, but you can easily leave out the alcohol.

DAIRY-FREE, NUT-FREE, UNDER 30 MINUTES

PREP TIME: 5 minutes, plus 5 minutes to marinate
TOTAL COOK TIME: 6 minutes

AIR CRISP: 6 minutes at 390°F

ACCESSORIES: Cook & Crisp™ basket

STORAGE: Store the shrimp in airtight containers in the refrigerator for up to 4 days or in the freezer for up to 2 months. Store tortillas and additional taco toppings in separate containers.

- **24 large shrimp, peeled and deveined**
- **2 tablespoons extra-virgin olive oil**
- **1 tablespoon tequila**
- **1 tablespoon freshly squeezed lime juice**
- **½ teaspoon chili powder**
- **½ teaspoon paprika**
- **½ teaspoon ground cumin**
- **½ teaspoon garlic powder**
- **¼ teaspoon onion powder**
- **¼ teaspoon kosher salt**
- **⅛ teaspoon freshly ground black pepper**
- **Nonstick cooking spray**
- **6 taco-size flour tortillas**
- **1 cup shredded lettuce**
- **2 or 3 thinly sliced radishes**
- **1 avocado, diced**
- **1 tablespoon chopped fresh cilantro**
- **Sour cream, guacamole, and pico de gallo, for serving (optional)**

1. Place the shrimp in a gallon-size resealable bag. Add the olive oil, tequila, lime juice, chili powder, paprika, cumin, garlic powder, onion powder, salt, and pepper. Massage the shrimp in the bag to coat it in the mixture. Set aside for 5 minutes to marinate. Do not marinate for much longer than 5 minutes because the lime will start to cook the shrimp.

2. Spray the Cook & Crisp™ basket with the cooking spray. Place the shrimp in the basket in a single layer, then lower the basket into the pot of your Ninja® Foodi™.

CONTINUED ▶

3. Select AIR CRISP, set the temperature to 390ºF, and set the time to 6 minutes. Select START/STOP to begin.

4. The shrimp is done cooking when it has turned pink and curled into a "c" shape. When cooking is complete, remove the basket from the Foodi™.

5. Let the shrimp cool to room temperature, then portion it into individual containers for the week; label and refrigerate or freeze. When ready to eat, assemble the tacos with the tortillas, lettuce, radishes, avocado, and cilantro. Serve with sour cream, guacamole, and/or pico de gallo salsa (if using).

Per serving: *Calories: 317; Total fat: 13g; Saturated fat: 2g; Cholesterol: 143mg; Sodium: 938mg; Carbohydrates: 29g; Fiber: 4g; Protein: 20g*

WEEK 6: BIG FLAVOR FAVES

When I'm meal prepping, I try to keep similar flavor profiles together because that helps cut down on shopping and prep times without repeating flavors too much. This week, we're letting spicy chorizo and savory tomato sauce take center stage in a variety of dishes.

SHOPPING LIST

Check your pantry for: nonstick cooking spray, extra-virgin olive oil, chicken broth, kosher salt, black pepper, dried oregano, paprika, and bay leaves.

VEGETABLES, HERBS, AND SPICES

- 1½ red bell peppers
- 2 small yellow onions
- 5 garlic cloves
- 2 cups sliced cremini or white button mushrooms
- 4 tablespoons chopped fresh parsley
- Pinch saffron threads

PROTEIN

- 4 fresh Mexican-style chorizo sausage links
- 1½ pounds boneless, skinless chicken thighs
- 1½ pounds bone-in, skin-on chicken thighs
- 6 large eggs

GRAINS

- 2 cups paella or Arborio rice

DAIRY

- ¼ cup heavy (whipping) cream or milk
- ⅓ cup shredded cheddar cheese

FROZEN

- ½ cup frozen peas

OTHER

- ½ cup dry white wine
- 1 (14.5-ounce) can stewed tomatoes
- 1 (14.5-ounce) can diced tomatoes
- 3 tablespoons tomato paste

MEAL PREP MENU

	BREAKFAST	LUNCH	DINNER
Day 1	Chorizo Egg Bites	Chicken and Chorizo Paella	Chicken Cacciatore served over rice
Day 2	Chorizo Egg Bites	Chicken Cacciatore served with a salad	Chicken and Chorizo Paella
Day 3	Chorizo Egg Bites	Chicken and Chorizo Paella	Chicken Cacciatore served over noodles
Day 4	Chorizo Egg Bites	Chicken Cacciatore served with garlic bread	Chicken and Chorizo Paella
Day 5	Chorizo Egg Bites	Chicken and Chorizo Paella	Chicken Cacciatore served over polenta

STEP-BY-STEP PREP

1. Chop 2 chorizo links into small bite-size pieces and set aside in a bowl for the **Chorizo Egg Bites** (page 82).

2. Cut 2 chorizo links into ½-inch slices and set aside in a bowl for **Chicken and Chorizo Paella** (page 87).

3. Chop the red bell peppers and divide into two bowls to use in the egg bites and the paella.

4. Dice the onions and mince the garlic, then divide into separate bowls for egg bites, paella, and **Chicken Cacciatore** (page 84).

5. Chop the parsley and set aside in a small bowl to use in the paella and cacciatore.

6. Fully prepare the **Chorizo Egg Bites**.

7. While the egg bites are steaming, chop the chicken and measure out the remaining ingredients for the **Chicken and Chorizo Paella**. Set aside.

8. When the egg bites are done cooking, let them cool to room temperature, then place them in an airtight container, label, and refrigerate or freeze. Wash the Foodi™ pot and wipe it dry.

9. Fully prepare the **Chicken and Chorizo Paella**. While the paella is cooking, slice the mushrooms and measure out the remaining ingredients for the **Chicken Cacciatore**.

10. When the paella is done cooking, let it cool to room temperature, portion it into airtight containers, label, and refrigerate or freeze. Wash the pot and wipe it dry.

11. Fully prepare the **Chicken Cacciatore**. When the recipe is done cooking, let it cool to room temperature, portion it into airtight containers, label, and refrigerate or freeze.

Chorizo Egg Bites

Starbucks made egg bites popular when they first introduced their Sous Vide Egg Bites in 2017, but those who have been following a low-carb, Whole30, or keto diet have known about them for way longer. I love egg bites because they're easy to customize with your favorite ingredients. In this recipe, the chorizo and red bell pepper add nice little kicks of heat and flavor, while the cream and cheese add the signature silkiness to the egg bites.

NUT-FREE

PREP TIME: 10 minutes
TOTAL COOK TIME:
29 minutes

**APPROX. PRESSURE
BUILD:** 10 minutes
PRESSURE COOK:
10 minutes
PRESSURE RELEASE:
natural for 5 minutes, then
quick

SAUTÉ: 4 minutes

ACCESSORIES: 2 Foodi™
mini molds or silicone
muffin molds, Deluxe
Reversible Rack

VARIATION TIP: Use
pepper Jack cheese or
habanero cheddar cheese
for spicy egg bites.

Nonstick cooking spray

**2 tablespoons
extra-virgin olive oil**

**2 fresh Mexican-style
chorizo links, cut
into small pieces**

½ red bell pepper, diced

½ small onion, finely diced

6 large eggs

**¼ cup heavy (whipping)
cream or milk**

¼ teaspoon kosher salt

**⅛ teaspoon freshly
ground black pepper**

**⅓ cup shredded
cheddar cheese**

1 cup water

1. Spray the cups of 2 mini molds with cooking spray and set aside.

2. Select SEAR/SAUTÉ on your Ninja® Foodi™, set the temperature to HI, and select START/STOP to begin.

3. Place the olive oil in the pot. Once the oil is hot, add the chorizo, red bell pepper, and onion and sauté for 3 to 4 minutes, just until the meat is cooked and the vegetables are softened. Select START/STOP. Transfer the chorizo and vegetables to a bowl and set aside. If there are browned bits at the bottom of the pot, wipe out the inside of the pot with a paper towel after it has cooled down.

4. In a large bowl, beat the eggs with the cream, salt, and pepper.

5. Divide the meat and vegetable mixture evenly among the cups of the mini molds (you will make 14 egg bites). Top with the cheese. Pour the egg mixture over the meat, leaving a little bit of room at the top because the eggs will puff up. Cover each mold with aluminum foil.

6. Pour the water into the pot. Place the Deluxe Reversible Rack in the lower steam position without the Deluxe Layer installed and lower it into the Foodi™ pot. Place one of the filled molds on the rack. Next, install the Deluxe Layer on the rack and place the remaining filled mold on it.

7. Assemble the pressure lid, making sure the pressure release valve is in the SEAL position. Select STEAM and set the time to 10 minutes. Select START/STOP to begin.

8. When cooking is complete, allow the pressure to release naturally for 5 minutes. After 5 minutes, quick release the remaining pressure by moving the pressure release valve to the VENT position. Carefully remove the lid when the unit has finished releasing pressure.

9. Let the egg bites cool to room temperature, then portion them into individual airtight containers for the week, label, and refrigerate or freeze.

STORAGE: Store in airtight containers in the refrigerator for up to 4 days or in the freezer for up to 2 months.

Per serving (2 bites): Calories: 231; Total fat: 20g; Saturated fat: 7g; Cholesterol: 192mg; Sodium: 406mg; Carbohydrates: 2g; Fiber: 1g; Protein: 11g

Chicken Cacciatore

A rich, rustic Italian dish of chicken in mushroom and tomato sauce, chicken cacciatore is best enjoyed with a table full of friends and family, a bottle of Italian wine, and crusty bread to soak up all of those delicious flavors in the sauce. It reheats beautifully, making it a tasty meal plan dish. For variety in your meal plan week, serve this with polenta, egg noodles, or rice.

DAIRY-FREE, GLUTEN-FREE, NUT-FREE

PREP TIME: 10 minutes
TOTAL COOK TIME:
26 minutes

APPROX. PRESSURE BUILD: 10 minutes
PRESSURE COOK:
11 minutes
PRESSURE RELEASE:
quick

SAUTÉ: 5 minutes

STORAGE: Store in airtight containers in the refrigerator for up to 4 days or in the freezer for up to 3 months.

- 1½ pounds bone-in, skin-on chicken thighs
- ½ teaspoon kosher salt
- ¼ teaspoon freshly ground black pepper
- 2 tablespoons extra-virgin olive oil
- 2 cups sliced cremini or white button mushrooms
- ½ small yellow onion, diced
- 2 garlic cloves, minced
- ½ teaspoon dried oregano
- ½ cup dry white wine
- ½ cup chicken stock
- 1 (14.5-ounce) can stewed tomatoes
- 3 tablespoons tomato paste
- 2 tablespoons chopped fresh parsley

1. Select SEAR/SAUTÉ on your Ninja® Foodi™ and set the temperature to HI. Select START/STOP to begin. Let preheat for 5 minutes.

2. Season the chicken with salt and pepper. Pour the olive oil into the pot. Once the oil is hot, add the chicken and cook for 5 to 6 minutes, stirring regularly to lightly brown the chicken. When the chicken is browned on all sides, transfer it to a plate.

3. Add the mushrooms, onion, garlic, and oregano and sauté for 3 to 4 minutes, just until the onion and garlic are soft and fragrant. Select START/STOP.

4. Slowly pour in the wine and use a wooden spoon to scrape up any browned bits at the bottom of the pot. Return the chicken to the pot. Pour in the chicken stock, tomatoes, and tomato paste.

5. Assemble the pressure lid, making sure the pressure release valve is in the SEAL position. Select PRESSURE and set it to HI. Set the time to 11 minutes. Select START/STOP to begin.

6. When pressure cooking is complete, quick release the pressure by turning the pressure release valve to the VENT position. Carefully remove the lid when the unit has finished releasing pressure.

7. Select SEAR/SAUTÉ and set the temperature to MD. Select START/STOP to begin.

8. Allow the sauce to come to a boil. Stir regularly for about 5 minutes, until the sauce has thickened.

9. Let the chicken, vegetables, and sauce cool at room temperature, then portion the dish into individual airtight containers for the week; label and refrigerate or freeze. When ready to eat, sprinkle with the parsley.

Per serving: Calories: 251; Total fat: 17g; Saturated fat: 4g; Cholesterol: 75mg; Sodium: 321mg; Carbohydrates: 7g; Fiber: 2g; Protein: 14g

Chicken and Chorizo Paella

SERVES 8

I love making this chicken and chorizo paella for meal plan weeks. It makes enough servings to enjoy for dinner and also for various meals for the next four days, or you can freeze half for later. You can use andouille sausage in place of chorizo, or if you prefer a mild paella, use sweet Italian sausage. The saffron threads help give paella its signature flavor and color, but you can use smoked or sweet paprika if you don't have saffron.

DAIRY-FREE, NUT-FREE

PREP TIME: 10 minutes
TOTAL COOK TIME:
32 minutes

APPROX. PRESSURE BUILD: 10 minutes
PRESSURE COOK:
5 minutes
PRESSURE RELEASE:
natural for 5 minutes, then quick

SAUTÉ: 7 minutes

STORAGE: Store in airtight containers in the refrigerator for up to 4 days or in the freezer for up to 3 months.

- 2 tablespoons extra-virgin olive oil
- 1½ pounds boneless, skinless chicken thighs, cut into 1-inch pieces
- 2 fresh Mexican-style chorizo links, cut into 1-inch diagonal slices
- 1 red bell pepper, seeded and diced
- 1 small yellow onion, diced
- 3 garlic cloves, minced
- ½ teaspoon paprika
- ½ teaspoon kosher salt
- ¼ teaspoon freshly ground black pepper
- 2 cups chicken stock
- Pinch saffron threads or ½ teaspoon smoked or sweet paprika
- 1 bay leaf
- 2 cups paella, Spanish (bomba), or Arborio rice
- 1 (14.5-ounce) can diced tomatoes
- ½ cup frozen peas
- 2 tablespoons chopped fresh parsley, for serving

1. Select SEAR/SAUTÉ on your Ninja® Foodi™ and set the temperature to HI. Select START/STOP to begin. Let preheat for 5 minutes.

2. Pour the oil into the pot. Once the oil is hot, add the chicken and sauté for about 2 minutes to brown it on all sides. Add the chorizo and sauté for 2 more minutes, then add the red pepper, onion, garlic, paprika, salt, and pepper and sauté for 2 more minutes. Select START/STOP.

CONTINUED ▶

3. Add the chicken stock, saffron, and bay leaf. Using a wooden spoon, scrape up any browned bits from the bottom of the pot. Add the rice and stir to combine. Add the tomatoes on top and gently press them down to submerge them in the liquid (do not stir).

4. Assemble the pressure lid, making sure the pressure release valve is in the SEAL position. Select PRESSURE and set it to HI. Set the time to 5 minutes. Select START/STOP to begin.

5. When cooking is complete, allow the pressure to naturally release for 10 minutes. After 10 minutes, quick release the remaining pressure by moving the pressure release valve to the VENT position. Carefully remove the lid when the unit has finished releasing pressure.

6. Immediately stir in the peas until they are heated through, about 1 minute. Remove and discard the bay leaf.

7. Let the paella cool to room temperature, then portion it into individual airtight containers for the week; label and refrigerate or freeze. When ready to eat, serve the paella sprinkled with parsley.

Per serving: Calories: 349; Total fat: 18g; Saturated fat: 5g; Cholesterol: 146mg; Sodium: 899mg; Carbohydrates: 13g; Fiber: 2g; Protein: 32g

WEEK 7: BETTER THAN TAKEOUT

This week, skip the takeout and make these popular dishes from scratch in the Foodi™. These recipes individually take less time to make than to place an order and wait for delivery. And they taste even better, too, because you can customize them exactly to your liking.

SHOPPING LIST

Check your pantry for: nonstick cooking spray, vegetable broth, granulated sugar, brown sugar, cornstarch, soy sauce, kosher salt, black pepper, and crushed red pepper flakes.

VEGETABLES, HERBS, AND SPICES

- 2 red bell peppers
- 2 or 3 fresh basil leaves
- 2 carrots
- 2 cups broccoli florets
- 1 small yellow onion
- 8 garlic cloves
- 2 tablespoons minced fresh ginger
- Scallions (optional)

PROTEIN

- 6 large eggs
- ½ pound ground breakfast sausage
- 24 slices pepperoni
- 24 slices salami
- 3 slices bacon
- 2 pounds boneless, skinless chicken thighs

GRAINS

- 6 (10-inch) flour tortillas
- 2 (7-inch) store-bought personal pizza crusts
- 8 ounces spaghetti

DAIRY

- 1 tablespoon unsalted butter
- 1 cup shredded cheddar cheese
- 1 cup shredded mozzarella cheese

OTHER

- ½ cup pizza sauce
- 1 tablespoon plus 1 teaspoon rice wine vinegar
- 1 teaspoon red chili paste
- 5 tablespoons sesame oil
- 1 cup plus 2 tablespoons orange juice
- Sesame seeds (optional)

MEAL PREP MENU

	BREAKFAST	LUNCH	DINNER
Day 1	Sausage and Egg Breakfast Burrito	Vegetable Lo Mein	Meat Lovers' Pizza
Day 2	Sausage and Egg Breakfast Burrito	Lightened-Up Orange Chicken served with salad	Vegetable Lo Mein
Day 3	Sausage and Egg Breakfast Burrito	Meat Lovers' Pizza	Lightened-Up Orange Chicken served over rice
Day 4	Sausage and Egg Breakfast Burrito	Meat Lovers' Pizza	Vegetable Lo Mein
Day 5	Sausage and Egg Breakfast Burrito	Lightened-Up Orange Chicken served with snap peas	Meat Lovers' Pizza

STEP-BY-STEP PREP

1. Dice the red bell peppers, then divide them into bowls according to the measurements for the **Sausage and Egg Breakfast Burritos** (page 92) and **Vegetable Lo Mein** (page 97).

2. Dice the onions and mince the garlic and ginger for the burritos, lo mein, and **Lightened-Up Orange Chicken** (page 99); and divide among bowls according to the recipes.

3. Fully prepare the **Sausage and Egg Breakfast Burritos**. While the burritos are crisping, prepare step 2 of the **Meat Lovers' Pizza** (page 95). Set the prepared pizzas aside.

4. When the burritos are done cooking, let them cool at room temperature. Wrap each burrito in aluminum foil, label, and refrigerate.

5. Wash and dry the Foodi™'s inner pot and the Deluxe Reversible Rack. Spray the racks with cooking spray, then continue with step 3 of the **Meat Lovers' Pizza** recipe.

6. While the pizzas are cooking, prepare the sauce in step 2 of the **Vegetable Lo Mein** recipe.

7. When the pizzas are done, let them cool at room temperature, then place slices into airtight containers; label and refrigerate.

8. If there are any sauce, cheese, or meat bits at the bottom of the pot, wipe the pot clean with a paper towel.

9. Prepare the **Vegetable Lo Mein** from step 3 through step 7.

10. While the lo mein is cooking, cut the chicken into 1-inch pieces for the **Lightened-Up Orange Chicken**. Set aside on a plate.

11. When lo mein is done cooking, let it cool at room temperature, portion it into airtight containers, label, and refrigerate or freeze.

12. Fully prepare the **Lightened-Up Orange Chicken** from step 2 through step 11. When the chicken is done cooking, let it cool at room temperature, then portion it into airtight containers, label, and refrigerate or freeze.

Sausage and Egg Breakfast Burrito

Instead of stopping by that fast-food joint on the way to work, fuel up with a homemade breakfast burrito—you can save money and time by making your own in the Foodi™. These are hearty, satisfying grab-and-go breakfasts the whole family will enjoy.

NUT-FREE, UNDER 30 MINUTES

PREP TIME: 10 minutes
TOTAL COOK TIME: 18 minutes

AIR CRISP: 10 minutes at 375°F

SAUTÉ: 8 minutes

ACCESSORIES: Deluxe Reversible Rack

VARIATION TIP: From this base recipe, try creating your own variations, such as a vegetarian burrito with sautéed broccoli and mushrooms. Or, switch up the meat and use bacon, chicken sausage, smoked salmon, or shrimp.

- 1 tablespoon unsalted butter
- 6 large eggs, lightly beaten
- ½ pound ground breakfast sausage
- ½ red bell pepper, diced
- 1 small yellow or white onion, diced
- ½ teaspoon kosher salt
- ¼ teaspoon freshly ground black pepper
- 6 (10-inch) flour tortillas
- 1 cup shredded cheddar cheese
- Nonstick cooking spray

1. Select SEAR/SAUTÉ on your Ninja® Foodi™ and set the temperature to MD:HI. Select START/STOP to begin. Let preheat for 5 minutes.

2. Place the butter in the pot and stir until melted. Add the eggs and scramble for 3 to 4 minutes, stirring regularly with a wooden spoon, until cooked. Transfer to a plate and set aside.

3. Add the sausage to the pot and sauté for 3 to 4 minutes, until no pink remains, stirring constantly to brown evenly. Add the bell pepper and onion, season with the salt and pepper, and sauté for 1 more minute.

4. Select START/STOP. Transfer the sausage and pepper mixture to a bowl.

5. Place one flour tortilla on a plate. Spoon 3 tablespoons of the sausage and pepper mixture and 2 to 3 tablespoons of scrambled eggs onto the center of the tortilla. Sprinkle 2 tablespoons of cheddar cheese over the filling. Fold the filled tortilla like a burrito, and secure it with a toothpick. Repeat until all burritos are assembled.

6. Use a paper towel to gently wipe up any oil or food remnants in the pot.

7. Lightly spray each burrito with cooking spray. Place the Deluxe Reversible Rack in the lower steam position without the Deluxe Layer installed, and lower the rack into the Foodi™ pot. Place 3 burritos on the rack. Next, install the Deluxe Layer on the rack and place the remaining burritos on it.

8. Close the crisping lid, select AIR CRISP, set the temperature to 375ºF, and set the time to 10 minutes. Select START/STOP to begin crisping.

9. After 5 minutes, to ensure even cooking, move the bottom burritos to the top rack and the top burritos to the bottom rack. Close the lid and continue cooking for 5 more minutes.

10. When cooking is complete, let the burritos cool at room temperature, then wrap each one in aluminum foil. Label and refrigerate.

STORAGE: Wrap in foil and refrigerate in airtight containers for up to 3 to 4 days. To reheat in the Foodi™, air crisp at 350°F for 2 minutes.

Per serving: Calories: 395; Total fat: 19g; Saturated fat: 8g; Cholesterol: 211mg; Sodium: 877mg; Carbohydrates: 30g; Fiber: 3g; Protein: 25g

Meat Lovers' Pizza

MAKES 2 PERSONAL PIZZAS

Does your family love pizza night as much as mine does? Save money and time by making your own personal pizzas in the Foodi™. This recipe is perfect for meal prep day and meal plan weeks because you can make it from start to finish in less than 20 minutes. That's it! Plus, it's easy to portion out for the week and can be enjoyed hot or cold.

NUT-FREE, UNDER
30 MINUTES

PREP TIME: 10 minutes
TOTAL COOK TIME:
8 minutes

BAKE/ROAST: 8 minutes
at 400°F

ACCESSORIES: Deluxe
Reversible Rack

VARIATION TIP: Use this
recipe as a jumping-off
point to try your own
pizza combos. Create
your own vegetarian
pizza, 5-cheese pizza, or
chicken-pesto pizza, for
example.

STORAGE: Wrap in
foil or place in airtight
containers and refrigerate
for up to 4 days.

2 (7-inch) store-bought
personal pizza crusts

½ cup pizza sauce

1 cup shredded
mozzarella cheese

24 slices pepperoni

24 slices salami

3 slices cooked
bacon, chopped

2 or 3 fresh basil leaves,
roughly torn

Crushed red pepper flakes,
for garnish (optional)

1. Select BAKE/ROAST on your Ninja® Foodi™, set the temperature to 400°F, and set the time to 5 minutes to preheat. Select START/STOP to begin.

2. Place each pizza crust on a separate plate. Spread the pizza sauce over the crusts, leaving a 1-inch border around the edges. Sprinkle the cheese evenly over each pizza. Top with the pepperoni, salami, and bacon.

3. Spray the Deluxe Reversible Rack with cooking spray. Place the Deluxe Reversible Rack in the lower steam position without the Deluxe Layer installed and lower the rack into the Foodi™ pot. Place one of the pizzas on the rack. Next, install the Deluxe Layer on the rack and place the remaining pizza on it. Close the crisping lid.

4. Select BAKE/ROAST, set the temperature to 400°F, and set the time to 8 minutes. Select START/STOP to begin.

CONTINUED ▶

Meat Lovers' Pizza continued

5. When the cooking is complete, carefully remove the pizzas from the Foodi™. Sprinkle the fresh basil leaves on the pizzas.

6. Let the pizzas cool at room temperature, then wrap them in aluminum foil or portion them into individual airtight containers for the week. Label and refrigerate. When ready to eat, garnish with red pepper flakes (if using).

Per serving: Calories: 797; Total fat: 48g; Saturated fat: 20g; Cholesterol: 145mg; Sodium: 1278mg; Carbohydrates: 45g; Fiber: 6g; Protein: 44g

Vegetable Lo Mein

Whenever my family ordered Chinese food takeout, we almost always ordered lo mein. But now, with the Foodi™, we can make these delectable noodles in less time than it takes to order and have it delivered. Use this vegetable lo mein recipe as a starting point to create different seafood and meat versions. Just toss in a cup of cooked meat or shrimp before serving.

DAIRY-FREE, NUT-FREE, UNDER 30 MINUTES, VEGAN

PREP TIME: 10 minutes
TOTAL COOK TIME: 15 minutes

APPROX. PRESSURE BUILD: 10 minutes
PRESSURE COOK: 5 minutes
PRESSURE RELEASE: quick

PREP TIP: You can chop the veggies and make the sauce one day ahead of time, then refrigerate until you are ready to cook.

STORAGE: Store in airtight containers in the refrigerator for up to 4 days or in the freezer for up to 2 months.

- 3 tablespoons toasted sesame oil, divided
- 2 carrots, julienned
- 1½ red bell peppers, diced
- 2 cups finely chopped broccoli florets
- 3 garlic cloves, minced
- 1 tablespoon minced fresh ginger
- 3 cups vegetable broth
- 2 tablespoons soy sauce
- 1 teaspoon rice wine vinegar
- 1 teaspoon brown sugar
- 1 teaspoon red chili paste
- 8 ounces spaghetti (or 3 ramen noodle packages, flavor packets discarded)
- Sliced scallions and sesame seeds, for serving (optional)

1. Select SEAR/SAUTÉ on your Ninja® Foodi™ and set the temperature to HI. Select START/STOP to begin. Preheat for 5 minutes.

2. Pour 2 tablespoons of sesame oil into the pot. Once the oil is hot, add the carrots, red bell peppers, and broccoli and sauté for 2 minutes. Mix in the garlic and ginger and sauté for 1 more minute. Select START/STOP.

CONTINUED ▶

3. Stir in the vegetable broth, soy sauce, vinegar, brown sugar, red chili paste, and remaining 1 tablespoon of sesame oil. Using a wooden spoon, scrape up any browned bits from the bottom of the pot. Place the spaghetti on top, breaking the pasta in half if necessary to fit lengthwise into the pot, and press down a bit to submerge as much of the pasta as possible in the liquid.

4. Assemble the pressure lid, making sure the pressure release valve is in the SEAL position. Select PRESSURE and set it to HI. Set the time to 5 minutes. Select START/STOP to begin.

5. When the pressure cooking is complete, quick release the pressure by turning the pressure release valve to the VENT position. Carefully remove the lid when the unit has finished releasing pressure.

6. Let the lo mein cool to room temperature, then portion it into individual airtight containers for the week. Label and refrigerate or freeze. Serve garnished with sliced scallions and sesame seeds (if using).

Per serving: Calories: 246; Total fat: 8g; Saturated fat: 1g; Cholesterol: 0mg; Sodium: 761mg; Carbohydrates: 38g; Fiber: 3g; Protein: 7g

Lightened-Up Orange Chicken

SERVES 6

A lighter riff on a popular Chinese food takeout dish, this Orange Chicken recipe skips the breading and frying and instead cooks the chicken directly in the sauce. Serve over rice or noodles, with a cucumber salad or mixed greens, or alongside sautéed green beans or snap peas.

DAIRY-FREE, NUT-FREE

PREP TIME: 10 minutes
TOTAL COOK TIME: 34 minutes

APPROX. PRESSURE BUILD: 10 minutes
PRESSURE COOK: 5 minutes
PRESSURE RELEASE: natural for 10 minutes, then quick

SAUTÉ: 9 minutes

STORAGE: Store in airtight containers in the refrigerator for up to 4 days or in the freezer for up to 3 months.

- 2 pounds boneless, skinless chicken thighs
- ½ teaspoon kosher salt
- ¼ teaspoon freshly ground black pepper
- 2 tablespoons sesame oil
- 1 tablespoon minced fresh ginger
- 5 garlic cloves, minced
- 1 cup plus 2 tablespoons freshly squeezed orange juice, divided
- 1 tablespoon rice wine vinegar
- ¼ cup soy sauce
- 1 tablespoon granulated sugar
- ¼ cup brown sugar
- 2 tablespoons cornstarch

1. Pat the chicken dry with paper towels, then cut it into 1-inch pieces. Season with the salt and pepper.

2. Select SEAR/SAUTÉ on your Ninja® Foodi™ and set the temperature to HI. Select START/STOP to begin.

3. Pour the sesame oil into the pot. Once the oil is hot, add the chicken and sauté for 3 to 4 minutes, just until the chicken is lightly browned on all sides. Add the ginger and garlic and sauté for 1 more minute. Select START/STOP.

4. Pour 1 cup of orange juice, the rice wine vinegar, soy sauce, granulated sugar, and brown sugar into the pot. Using a wooden spoon, scrape up any browned bits from the bottom of the pot.

CONTINUED ▶

5. Assemble the pressure lid, making sure the pressure release valve is in the SEAL position. Select PRESSURE and set it to HI. Set the time to 5 minutes. Select START/STOP to begin.

6. While the chicken is cooking, in a medium bowl, whisk together the cornstarch and remaining 2 tablespoons of orange juice until smooth. Set aside.

7. When the pressure cooking is complete, allow the pressure to release naturally for 10 minutes. After 10 minutes, quick release the remaining pressure by moving the pressure release valve to the VENT position. Carefully remove the lid when the unit has finished releasing pressure.

8. Select SEAR/SAUTÉ and set the temperature to HI. Select START/STOP to begin.

9. Pour in the cornstarch-orange juice mixture and stir to combine. Stir occasionally, as the sauce thickens, for about 5 minutes. Select START/STOP.

10. Let the chicken and sauce cool at room temperature, then portion them into individual airtight containers for the week. Label and refrigerate or freeze.

Per serving: Calories: 307; Total fat: 11g; Saturated fat: 2g; Cholesterol: 142mg; Sodium: 829mg; Carbohydrates: 20g; Fiber: 0g; Protein: 31g

WEEK 8: AROUND THE WORLD

One of the best aspects of travel is learning about and trying new dishes. This week, take a trip around the world through your tastebuds. Incorporating foods from a variety of different cultures is one way to keep meal prep interesting and oh so delicious.

SHOPPING LIST

Check your pantry for: extra-virgin olive oil, vegetable broth, chicken broth, all-purpose flour, kosher salt, black pepper, paprika, cumin, turmeric, curry powder, cayenne pepper, cumin, and dried thyme.

FRUIT, VEGETABLES, HERBS, AND SPICES

- 1 red bell pepper
- 3 cups sliced cremini or white button mushrooms
- 3½ small yellow onions
- 10 garlic cloves
- 1 tablespoon plus 1 teaspoon minced fresh ginger
- ¼ cup chopped fresh parsley
- ¼ cup plus 2 tablespoons chopped fresh cilantro
- 1 teaspoon fresh thyme
- 1 lime
- ½ cup dried cherries or dried apricots

PROTEIN

- 1½ pounds large shrimp
- 2 pounds boneless, skinless chicken thighs
- 6 large eggs

GRAINS

- 12 ounces wide egg noodles
- 1 cup quinoa
- 2 cups basmati rice

DAIRY

- 3 tablespoons unsalted butter
- ½ cup sour cream

OTHER

- ¼ cup white wine
- 1 tablespoon Worcester-shire sauce
- 1 (14.5-ounce) can chickpeas
- 2 (15-ounce) cans crushed tomatoes
- 1 tablespoon tomato paste

MEAL PREP MENU

	BREAKFAST	LUNCH	DINNER
Day 1	Shakshuka	Moroccan-Inspired Chicken and Chickpeas with Quinoa	Mushroom Stroganoff
Day 2	Shakshuka	Indian-Inspired Shrimp Biryani	Moroccan-inspired Chicken and Chickpeas with Quinoa
Day 3	Shakshuka	Mushroom Stroganoff	Indian-Inspired Shrimp Biryani
Day 4	Shakshuka	Moroccan-Inspired Chicken and Chickpeas with Quinoa	Mushroom Stroganoff
Day 5	Shakshuka	Indian-Inspired Shrimp Biryani	Moroccan-Inspired Chicken and Chickpeas with Quinoa

STEP-BY-STEP PREP

1. Dice the onions and mince the garlic and ginger. Divide among bowls based on the measurements for each of this week's recipes.

2. Fully prepare the **Mushroom Stroganoff** (page 104).

3. While the **Mushroom Stroganoff** is cooking, drain and rinse the chickpeas for the **Moroccan-Inspired Chicken and Chickpeas with Quinoa** (page 107). Set aside in a bowl. Continue with steps 2 and 3 in measuring and prepping ingredients for the Moroccan Chicken.

4. When the **Mushroom Stroganoff** is done cooking, let it cool to room temperature, then portion it into airtight containers, label, and refrigerate or freeze. Wash the pot and wipe it dry.

5. Prepare the rest of the **Moroccan-Inspired Chicken and Chickpeas with Quinoa** recipe, steps 4 through 10.

6. While the chicken is cooking, prepare the ingredients in step 2 of the **Indian-Inspired Shrimp Biryani** recipe (page 109). Then, measure out and set aside the remaining ingredients for this recipe.

7. When the chicken is done cooking, let it cool at room temperature, then portion it into airtight containers, label, and refrigerate.

8. Prepare the **Indian-Inspired Shrimp Biryani**, steps 3 through 10. When the recipe is done cooking, let it cool at room temperature, then portion it into airtight containers, label, and refrigerate. Wash the pot and wipe it dry.

9. Fully prepare the **Shakshuka** (page 111) through step 8. When it has finished cooking, let the recipe cool at room temperature, then very carefully transfer the eggs and sauce into airtight containers, label, and refrigerate.

Mushroom Stroganoff

SERVES 6

Beef Stroganoff is a popular Russian dish named after an eighteenth-century noble. If you've never had the traditional version, it's typically a beef dish with a luscious sour cream sauce. This vegetarian version is every bit as hearty and satisfying as the traditional meaty version, and it's a mushroom lover's dream dish.

NUT-FREE

PREP TIME: 5 minutes
TOTAL COOK TIME:
23 minutes

APPROX. PRESSURE
BUILD: 10 minutes
PRESSURE COOK:
3 minutes
PRESSURE RELEASE:
quick

SAUTÉ: 10 minutes

3 tablespoons
  unsalted butter

½ small yellow onion, diced

3 garlic cloves, minced

3 cups sliced cremini or
  white button mushrooms

½ teaspoon paprika

½ teaspoon kosher salt

¼ teaspoon freshly
  ground black pepper

3 tablespoons
  all-purpose flour

¼ cup white wine

3 cups vegetable
  broth or water

1 tablespoon
  Worcestershire sauce

1 teaspoon fresh thyme or
  ½ teaspoon dried thyme

12 ounces wide
  egg noodles

½ cup sour cream

¼ cup chopped
  fresh parsley

1. Select SEAR/SAUTÉ on your Ninja® Foodi™ and set the temperature to HI. Select START/STOP to begin.

2. Place the butter in the pot. When the butter is completely melted, add the onion, garlic, mushrooms, paprika, salt, and pepper and sauté for 5 minutes.

3. Sprinkle the flour over the vegetables and stir to combine. Pour in the wine and use a wooden spoon to scrape up any browned bits at the bottom of the pot. Select START/STOP.

4. Stir in the broth, Worcestershire sauce, and thyme. Place the noodles in the pot, spreading them out evenly, and gently press them down to submerge them in the liquid. It's okay if some pasta is above the liquid.

5. Assemble the pressure lid, making sure the pressure release valve is in the SEAL position. Select PRESSURE and set it to HI. Set the time to 3 minutes. Select START/STOP to begin.

6. When the pressure cooking is complete, quick release the pressure by turning the pressure release valve to the VENT position. Carefully remove the lid when the unit has finished releasing pressure.

7. Select SEAR/SAUTÉ and set the temperature to HI. Select START/STOP to begin. Stir in the sour cream and allow the sauce to thicken for 3 to 5 minutes.

8. Let the mushroom Stroganoff cool to room temperature, then portion it into individual airtight containers for the week. Label and refrigerate or freeze. When ready to eat, garnish with the parsley.

Per serving: Calories: 344; Total fat: 12g; Saturated fat: 7g; Cholesterol: 73mg; Sodium: 151mg; Carbohydrates: 47g; Fiber: 3g; Protein: 10g

STORAGE: Store in airtight containers in the refrigerator for up to 4 days or in the freezer for up to 1 month. To reheat in the Foodi™, select SEAR/SAUTÉ, set the temperature to HI, and select START/STOP to begin. Add a portion to the pot, along with 1 tablespoon of extra-virgin olive oil and 1 tablespoon of water. Stir to combine, then continue stirring until the mushroom Stroganoff is heated through, 2 to 3 minutes. To reheat in the microwave, place one serving in a microwave-safe bowl, add 1 tablespoon of water or milk, and then reheat in 45-second increments until hot.

Moroccan-Inspired Chicken and Chickpeas with Quinoa

SERVES 6

This fragrant, flavorful dish is inspired by Moroccan tagine, a stew-like dish typically made with chicken or lamb and dried fruit and served over couscous. The Foodi™ allows the aromatic spices to infuse the chicken quickly, resulting in a slow-cooked consistency and taste. You can use almost any dried fruit—I like the cherries in this recipe, but apricots and golden raisins are equally delicious. I use quinoa in my version to make this a nutritious one-dish meal.

DAIRY-FREE, GLUTEN-FREE, NUT-FREE

PREP TIME: 10 minutes
TOTAL COOK TIME: 30 minutes

APPROX. PRESSURE BUILD: 10 minutes
PRESSURE COOK: 10 minutes
PRESSURE RELEASE: quick

SAUTÉ: 10 minutes

VARIATION TIP: You can substitute Israeli couscous for the quinoa.

STORAGE: Store in airtight containers in the refrigerator for up to 4 days or in the freezer for up to 3 months.

- 1 teaspoon paprika
- 1 teaspoon ground turmeric
- 1 teaspoon ground cumin
- ½ teaspoon kosher salt
- ¼ teaspoon freshly ground black pepper
- 2 pounds boneless, skinless chicken thighs
- 3 tablespoons extra-virgin olive oil, divided
- 2 garlic cloves, minced
- 1 small yellow onion, diced
- 1 teaspoon minced fresh ginger
- 1 cup quinoa
- ½ cup dried cherries or chopped dried apricots
- 1 (14.5-ounce) can chickpeas, drained and rinsed
- 1 (14.5-ounce) can chicken broth
- Finely chopped fresh cilantro or parsley, for serving (optional)

1. Select SEAR/SAUTÉ on your Ninja® Foodi™ and set the temperature to HI. Select START/STOP to begin. Let preheat for 5 minutes.

2. Meanwhile, in a small bowl, stir together the paprika, turmeric, cumin, salt, and pepper.

3. Coat the chicken with the spice rub as evenly as possible on both sides. Set aside on a plate.

CONTINUED ▶

4. Pour 2 tablespoons of olive oil into the pot. Once the oil is hot, add the chicken and cook for 2 to 3 minutes on each side, just until slightly browned. Transfer the chicken to a plate and set aside.

5. Add the remaining 1 tablespoon of olive oil to the pot. Once the oil is hot, add the garlic, onion, and ginger and sauté for 2 minutes, just until the vegetables are soft and fragrant. Add the quinoa, dried cherries, chickpeas, chicken broth, and the browned chicken.

6. Assemble the pressure lid, making sure the pressure release valve is in the SEAL position. Select PRESSURE and set it to HI. Set the time to 5 minutes. Select START/STOP to begin.

7. When the pressure cooking is complete, quick release the pressure by turning the pressure release valve to the VENT position. Carefully remove the lid when the unit has finished releasing pressure. Cooking is complete when the internal temperature of the meat reads at least 165°F on a food thermometer.

8. Let the chicken cool to room temperature, then portion it into individual airtight containers for the week. Label and refrigerate or freeze. When ready to eat, serve with cilantro (if using).

Per serving: *Calories: 440; Total fat: 16g; Saturated fat: 3g; Cholesterol: 144mg; Sodium: 605mg; Carbohydrates: 36g; Fiber: 6g; Protein: 38g*

Indian-Inspired Shrimp Biryani

This rustic meat and rice dish originated in Persia and traveled to India, where it became a beloved and widely shared dish. You'll find biryani made with all sorts of meat and seafood; I use shrimp in my version because they stand up to the big flavors in the dish but have short cook and prep times.

DAIRY-FREE, NUT-FREE, UNDER 30 MINUTES

PREP TIME: 5 minutes
TOTAL COOK TIME:
21 minutes

APPROX. PRESSURE
BUILD: 10 minutes
PRESSURE COOK:
3 minutes
PRESSURE RELEASE:
natural for 5 minutes, then quick

SAUTÉ: 8 minutes

1½ pounds large shrimp, peeled and deveined

1 teaspoon curry powder, divided

1 teaspoon kosher salt, divided

½ teaspoon freshly ground black pepper, divided

5 tablespoons extra-virgin olive oil, divided

1 small yellow onion, diced

1 tablespoon minced fresh ginger

3 garlic cloves, minced

1 teaspoon paprika

¼ teaspoon cayenne pepper

1 teaspoon ground turmeric

2 cups basmati rice

2½ cups water

¼ cup chopped fresh cilantro, for serving

1 lime, cut into wedges, for serving

1. Select SEAR/SAUTÉ on your Ninja® Foodi™ and set the temperature to HI. Select START/STOP to begin. Let preheat for 5 minutes.

2. In a large bowl, toss together the shrimp, ½ teaspoon of curry powder, ½ teaspoon of salt, and ¼ teaspoon of black pepper.

3. Pour 2 tablespoons of olive oil into the Foodi™ pot. Once the oil is hot, add the shrimp and sauté for 3 to 4 minutes, just until the shrimp starts to change color but is not completely cooked. Transfer the shrimp to a bowl.

CONTINUED ▶

Indian-Inspired Shrimp Biryani continued

continued

STORAGE: Store in airtight containers in the refrigerator for up to 4 days or in the freezer for up to 3 months. To reheat in the Foodi™, select SEAR/SAUTÉ, set the temperature to HI, and select START/STOP to begin. Add a portion to the pot, along with 1 tablespoon of extra-virgin olive oil and 1 tablespoon of water. Stir until the biryani is heated through, 2 to 3 minutes. To reheat in the microwave, place one serving in a microwave-safe bowl, add 1 tablespoon of water (this helps "wake up" the rice with added moisture), and then reheat in 45-second increments until hot.

4. Add the remaining 3 tablespoons of olive oil to the Foodi™ pot. Once the oil is hot, add the onion, ginger, garlic, paprika, cayenne, turmeric, and remaining ½ teaspoon of curry powder; sauté for 1 to 2 minutes, just until the onion and garlic are soft and fragrant. Select START/STOP.

5. Add the rice, water, remaining ½ teaspoon of salt and ¼ teaspoon of black pepper to the pot and stir to combine.

6. Assemble the pressure lid, making sure the pressure release valve is in the SEAL position. Select PRESSURE and set it to HI. Set the time to 3 minutes. Select START/STOP to begin.

7. When the pressure cooking is complete, quick release the pressure by turning the pressure release valve to the VENT position. Carefully remove the lid when the unit has finished releasing pressure.

8. Select SEAR/SAUTÉ and set the temperature to HI. Select START/STOP to begin. Return the shrimp to the pot and stir it into the rice for 1 to 2 minutes, just until the shrimp turns opaque and is completely cooked.

9. Let the shrimp and rice cool to room temperature, then portion them into individual airtight containers for the week. Label and refrigerate or freeze. When ready to eat, serve with chopped cilantro and lime wedges.

Per serving: Calories: 426; Total fat: 13g; Saturated fat: 2g; Cholesterol: 143mg; Sodium: 838mg; Carbohydrates: 55g; Fiber: 2g; Protein: 20g

Shakshuka

Although this robust, saucy tomato and egg dish is said to have originated in North Africa, its many variations are most popular these days throughout the Middle East. In North America, you'll often find it served for brunch, and it's usually offered in red and/or green varieties. This recipe is for a red shakshuka, and it's an amazing dish to enjoy any time of day.

DAIRY-FREE, GLUTEN-FREE, NUT-FREE

PREP TIME: 10 minutes
TOTAL COOK TIME: 32 minutes

APPROX. PRESSURE BUILD: 10 minutes
PRESSURE COOK: 5 minutes
PRESSURE RELEASE: quick

SAUTÉ: 11 minutes

BROIL: 6 minutes

PREP TIP: Because this tomato dish has strong aromas and flavors, make it last on meal prep days. That way, you can give the pot and pressure cooker lid an extra-thorough wash and proper time to fully dry out before using them for other recipes.

¼ cup plus 2 tablespoons extra-virgin olive oil, divided

1 red bell pepper, diced

1 small yellow onion, diced

2 garlic cloves, minced

2 (15-ounce) cans crushed tomatoes

1 tablespoon tomato paste

2 teaspoons paprika

2 teaspoons ground cumin

½ teaspoon kosher salt

6 large eggs

2 tablespoons chopped fresh cilantro

1. Select SEAR/SAUTÉ on your Ninja® Foodi™ and set the temperature to HI. Select START/STOP to begin. Let preheat for 5 minutes.

2. Pour 2 tablespoons of olive oil into the pot. Once the oil is hot, add the red bell pepper, onion, and garlic and sauté for 2 minutes, just until the vegetables are soft and fragrant. Stir in the tomatoes, tomato paste, paprika, cumin, remaining ¼ cup of olive oil, and salt.

3. Assemble the pressure lid, making sure the pressure release valve is in the SEAL position. Select PRESSURE and set it to HI. Set the time to 5 minutes. Select START/STOP to begin.

4. When the pressure cooking is complete, quick release the pressure by turning the pressure release valve to the VENT position. Carefully remove the lid when the unit has finished releasing pressure.

CONTINUED ▶

Shakshuka continued

STORAGE: To store individual servings for meal prep, use a large ladle to very carefully scoop out individual eggs and place them in storage containers. Then, scoop out the vegetable sauce and pour it over and around the eggs in each container. Refrigerate for up to 4 days.

5. Select SEAR/SAUTÉ and set the temperature to MD. Select START/STOP to begin. Stir the vegetables until they have fully softened, 3 to 4 minutes. With a wooden spoon, create little wells within the sauce for the eggs. Very carefully break an egg over each well, taking care not to break the yolk. Alternatively, you can break the eggs into individual ramekins first, then carefully slide each egg from the ramekin into the well in the sauce.

6. Close the crisping lid. Set to BROIL and set the time to 6 minutes. Select START/STOP to begin. Cook until the whites of each egg are set.

7. Let the shakshuka cool to room temperature, then portion it into individual airtight containers for the week. Label and refrigerate. When you're ready to eat the shakshuka, sprinkle the cilantro over the top.

Per serving: Calories: 256; Total fat: 19g; Saturated fat: 3g; Cholesterol: 186mg; Sodium: 437mg; Carbohydrates: 14g; Fiber: 4g; Protein: 9g

Chocolate-Hazelnut Croissants, *page 124*

3

BREAKFAST AND BRUNCH

Garlic-Rosemary Breakfast Potatoes

SERVES 6

Breakfast potatoes are perfect for meal planning. My whole family loves them because we can each add a twist to leftovers. You can enjoy them on their own or add your favorite breakfast protein; I'll even eat them cold. Try adding a poached or fried egg, bacon, sausage, smoked salmon, or sautéed vegetables. Turn leftovers into a hearty dinner by baking them into a casserole.

DAIRY-FREE, GLUTEN-FREE, NUT-FREE, UNDER 30 MINUTES, VEGAN

PREP TIME: 10 minutes
TOTAL COOK TIME: 15 minutes

AIR CRISP: 15 minutes at 400°F

ACCESSORIES: Cook & Crisp™ basket

PREP TIP: To reheat leftover potatoes so they retain their crispiness, place them in the Cook & Crisp™ basket in your Ninja® Foodi™, select AIR CRISP, set the temperature to 375°F, and set the time to 5 minutes.

STORAGE: Store in airtight containers in the refrigerator for up to 4 days or in the freezer for up to 2 months.

1 tablespoon extra-virgin olive oil

4 large baking potatoes, cut into small cubes

2 garlic cloves, minced

1 tablespoon chopped fresh rosemary

½ teaspoon kosher salt

¼ teaspoon freshly ground black pepper

1. Insert the Cook & Crisp™ basket in the pot of your Ninja® Foodi™ and close the crisping lid. Select AIR CRISP, set the temperature to 375°F, and set the time to 5 minutes. Select START/STOP to begin preheating.

2. Meanwhile, in a large bowl, toss together the olive oil, potatoes, garlic, and rosemary until the potatoes are well coated. Season with the salt and pepper.

3. When the Foodi™ has finished preheating, open the crisping lid and gently place the potatoes in the basket.

4. Close the crisping lid. Select AIR CRISP, set the temperature to 400°F, and set the time to 15 minutes. Select START/STOP to begin. After 8 minutes, open the lid and use a wooden spoon to gently toss the potatoes, moving the potatoes on the bottom to the top for even crisping. Close the lid to resume cooking for the remaining 7 minutes.

5. When cooking is complete, check the potatoes for your desired crispiness. Remove the potatoes from the basket and let them cool to room temperature. Divide the potatoes among individual containers, label, and refrigerate or freeze.

Per serving: Calories: 215; Total fat: 3g; Saturated fat: 0g; Cholesterol: 0mg; Sodium: 125mg; Carbohydrates: 43g; Fiber: 5g; Protein: 5g

Fruit and Granola Yogurt Parfaits

Homemade yogurt is so satisfying: it's healthier (less sugar) and costs less than store-bought yogurt. This is one breakfast that is best to start the night before your meal prep day. Start the process after dinner so the milk has a chance to cool and is ready for the yogurt starter before bedtime. Then, let it ferment overnight, and in the morning, you'll have a big batch of fresh, delicious yogurt— perfect for layering with granola and your favorite mixed berries to enjoy as nutritious breakfast parfaits all week long.

VEGETARIAN

PREP TIME: 5 minutes, plus 8 hours to ferment
TOTAL TIME: 12 hours

PREP TIP: Be sure to use fresh, plain yogurt that says "live, active cultures" on the packaging. Active cultures, or bacteria, are what turn the milk into yogurt during fermentation.

STORAGE: Refrigerate in airtight containers for up to 2 weeks.

2 quarts whole milk

2 tablespoons plain yogurt with active live cultures

1 tablespoon vanilla extract (optional)

½ cup honey (optional)

1 cup Cinnamon-Almond Granola (page 49) or store-bought granola

2 cups mixed berries (such as blueberries, raspberries, strawberries, or blackberries)

1. Pour the milk into the inner pot of your Ninja® Foodi™. Assemble the pressure lid, making sure the pressure release valve is in the VENT position. Select YOGURT. The time should automatically display 8 minutes. Select START/STOP to begin.

2. The Foodi™ will bring the milk to a boil. This takes between 30 minutes and 1 hour. Once the milk reaches a boil, the unit will beep and automatically display COOL. The Foodi™ will then allow the milk to cool, which may take anywhere from 1 to 3 hours.

3. Once the milk has cooled, the Foodi™ will beep and display ADD AND STIR. Carefully open the pressure lid. Whisk in the yogurt until it is fully incorporated. Assemble the pressure lid, making sure the pressure release valve is in the VENT position. The screen should now display FMNT with a time set to 8 hours. Let ferment, undisturbed, for 8 hours.

4. After 8 hours, transfer the yogurt to a large glass container or bowl, cover, and chill for 4 hours in the refrigerator.

5. Stir in the vanilla and honey (if using).

6. Spoon the yogurt into two large glass jars or other airtight containers; label and refrigerate. When ready to eat, spoon a layer of yogurt into a bowl, top with a layer of granola, and then add a layer of berries. Repeat the layers to create individual parfaits.

Per serving: Calories: 274; Total fat: 11g; Saturated fat: 6g; Cholesterol: 33mg; Sodium: 144mg; Carbohydrates: 33g; Fiber: 3g; Protein: 12g

Blackberry Toaster Pastries

These nostalgic toaster pastries from my childhood are now fun for my own kids to help make and enjoy. These pastries are perfect for when you want to add a fun morning treat to your meal plan. You can substitute any flavor of preserves for the blackberry, and you can choose to go without the icing and sprinkles if you prefer—although my kids think the icing and sprinkles are the best parts.

DAIRY-FREE, NUT-FREE, UNDER 30 MINUTES

PREP TIME: 5 minutes
TOTAL COOK TIME: 10 minutes

AIR CRISP: 10 minutes at 350°F

ACCESSORIES: Deluxe Reversible Rack

STORAGE: Place in an airtight container with parchment paper or wax paper between each pastry, and store at room temperature for up to 5 days.

1 (14.1-ounce) package refrigerated piecrusts (two 9-inch crusts)

¼ cup blackberry preserves

1 large egg

1 teaspoon water

Nonstick cooking spray

1 cup powdered sugar

2 teaspoons freshly squeezed lemon juice, plus more as needed

Sprinkles, for decorating

1. Unroll both piecrusts. Stack one on top of the other, and cut off the rounded sides so that you are left with two large (9-by-9-inch) squares. Lay the squares side by side on your work surface, and cut each square into 6 (3-by-4.5-inch) rectangles for a total of 12 rectangles. Lay 6 rectangles flat on your work surface; set the others aside.

2. Spoon 2 teaspoons of blackberry preserves onto the center of each of the 6 rectangles.

3. In a small bowl, beat together the egg and water to make an egg wash. Brush the inside edges of each rectangle with the mixture.

4. Top with the remaining rectangles of dough. Using your fingers, press down around the edges of each pastry, removing as much air as possible. Using the tines of a fork, press down on the edges of each pastry to further secure the tops to the bottoms. Then, use the tines of a fork to poke a few small holes into the center of the top layer of each pastry. Brush the tops with the egg wash.

5. Spray the Deluxe Reversible Rack with cooking spray. Place the Deluxe Reversible Rack in the lower steam position without the Deluxe Layer installed and lower the rack into the Foodi™ pot. Place 3 toaster pastries on the rack. Next, install the Deluxe Layer on the rack and place the remaining toaster pastries on it.

6. Close the crisping lid. Select AIR CRISP, set the temperature to 350ºF, and set the time to 10 minutes. Select START/STOP to begin.

7. When cooking is complete, open the crisping lid and carefully remove the rack. Let the pastries cool on the racks.

8. While the pastries cool, in a medium bowl, whisk together the powdered sugar and lemon juice until smooth. Add more lemon juice as needed, 1 teaspoon at a time, to create a smooth icing.

9. Spread about 1 tablespoon of icing on top of each pastry. While the icing is still wet, shake the sprinkles over the icing. Let the pastries cool and set for 1 to 2 minutes before serving or storing.

Per serving: *Calories: 436; Total fat: 20g; Saturated fat: 8g; Cholesterol: 31mg; Sodium: 325mg; Carbohydrates: 60g; Fiber: 2g; Protein: 3g*

Sausage and Spinach Frittata

SERVES 6

This frittata is a versatile, hearty breakfast dish that allows you to use up any leftover meats and vegetables you might have on hand. In particular, feel free to sub in bacon, ground beef, mushrooms, broccoli, or other melty cheeses. A 7-inch baking pan or baking dish fits nicely in the Foodi™.

GLUTEN-FREE, NUT-FREE

PREP TIME: 5 minutes
TOTAL COOK TIME:
29 minutes

APPROX. PRESSURE
BUILD: 7 minutes
PRESSURE COOK:
12 minutes
PRESSURE RELEASE:
natural for 10 minutes,
then quick

AIR CRISP (OPTIONAL):
5 minutes at 375°F

ACCESSORIES: Deluxe
Reversible Rack, Foodi™
all-purpose pan

Nonstick cooking spray

1 teaspoon extra-virgin
 olive oil

8 ounces ground
 breakfast sausage
 or Italian sausage

½ cup finely chopped onion

½ cup chopped red
 bell pepper

1 cup water

6 large eggs

1 cup chopped baby
 spinach leaves

½ cup shredded
 cheddar cheese

½ teaspoon kosher salt

¼ teaspoon freshly
 ground black pepper

1. Spray a Foodi™ all-purpose pan with cooking spray, then line the bottom with parchment paper. Set aside.

2. Select SEAR/SAUTÉ on your Ninja® Foodi™ and set the temperature to HI. Select START/STOP to begin. Let preheat for 5 minutes.

3. Pour the olive oil into the pot. Once the oil is hot, add the sausage and cook, stirring occasionally, for 3 to 4 minutes, until browned. Add the onion and bell pepper and sauté for 1 to 2 minutes, until the vegetables have softened. Transfer the sausage and vegetables to a plate or bowl and set aside.

4. Wipe the Foodi™'s inner pot clean with a paper towel, and pour in the water.

5. In a large bowl, whisk the eggs until they are well blended. Add the spinach, cheese, salt, and pepper to the eggs and stir to combine. Stir in the sausage mixture.

6. Pour the egg mixture into the prepared all-purpose pan. Cover tightly with aluminum foil.

7. Place the Deluxe Reversible Rack in the lower steam position without the Deluxe Layer installed and lower the rack into the Foodi™ pot. Place the filled all-purpose pan on the rack.

8. Assemble the pressure lid, making sure the pressure release valve is in the SEAL position. Select PRESSURE and set it to HI. Set the time to 12 minutes. Select START/STOP to begin.

9. When the pressure cooking is complete, allow the pressure to naturally release for 10 minutes. After 10 minutes, quick release remaining pressure by moving the pressure release valve to the VENT position. Carefully remove the lid when the unit has finished releasing pressure, and lift the pan from the pot. Slice and serve the frittata while it's still warm, or let it cool to room temperature, divide it into airtight containers, and refrigerate or freeze.

Per serving: Calories: 266; Total fat: 21g; Saturated fat: 8g; Cholesterol: 224mg; Sodium: 525mg; Carbohydrates: 4g; Fiber: 1g; Protein: 15g

PREP TIP: I like my frittata lightly browned on top. After pressure cooking, remove the Deluxe Reversible Rack and all-purpose pan from the pot. Pour out all liquid in the pot, remove the foil from the frittata, then return the rack and pan to the pot. Close the crisping lid. Select AIR CRISP, set temperature to 375°F, and set time to 5 minutes. Select START/STOP to begin. When cooking is complete, open crisping lid and remove the all-purpose pan.

STORAGE: Wrap leftover frittata slices in plastic wrap, then place them in separate airtight containers. Refrigerate for up to 4 days or freeze for up to 2 months.

Chocolate-Hazelnut Croissants

If you're a fan of chocolate-hazelnut spread or chocolate croissants, you'll love this easy breakfast pastry recipe. It only requires two ingredients: refrigerated crescent dough and your favorite chocolate-hazelnut spread. Because you're not spending all day making the dough from scratch, this is a great recipe to make on your meal prep day.

UNDER 30 MINUTES, VEGETARIAN

PREP TIME: 5 minutes
TOTAL COOK TIME: 8 minutes

AIR CRISP: 8 minutes at 325°F

ACCESSORIES: Deluxe Reversible Rack

STORAGE: Wrap in aluminum foil and refrigerate in an airtight container for up to 3 to 4 days. To reheat, place the Deluxe Reversible Rack in the pot and close the crisping lid. Select AIR CRISP, set the temperature to 325°F, and set the time to 2 minutes. Select START/STOP to begin.

1 (8-ounce) can refrigerated crescent dough

½ cup to 1 cup of chocolate-hazelnut spread, plus more for drizzling (optional)

1. Close the crisping lid on your Ninja® Foodi™. Select AIR CRISP, set the temperature to 325°F, and set the time to 5 minutes. Select START/STOP to begin preheating.

2. Unroll the crescent dough and separate it along the precut lines into 8 triangles. Place one tablespoon of chocolate-hazelnut spread in the middle of the widest edge of each triangle, then roll each one into the shape of a croissant with the final triangle corner on top. Gently curve the ends of each croissant inward to form a crescent shape.

3. Once the Foodi™ has preheated, spray the Deluxe Reversible Rack with cooking spray. Place the Deluxe Reversible Rack in the lower steam position without the Deluxe Layer installed and lower the rack into the Foodi™ pot. Place 4 croissants on the rack. Next, install the Deluxe Layer on the rack and place the remaining croissants on it.

4. Close the crisping lid. Select AIR CRISP, set the temperature to 325°F, and set the time to 8 minutes. Select START/STOP to begin.

5. After 4 minutes, open the lid and use oven mitts to lift the rack out of the Foodi™ pot. Using tongs, move the top croissants to the bottom rack and the bottom croissants to the top rack. Carefully lower the rack back into the Foodi™ pot. Close the lid and continue cooking for 4 more minutes, until the croissants are golden brown.

6. Optional: To decorate, melt ½ cup chocolate-hazelnut spread in the microwave for 30 seconds. Spoon the heated chocolate into a plastic zip-top bag, snip off one corner, and squeeze the spread over each croissant.

Per serving (1 croissant): Calories: 187; Total fat: 9g; Saturated fat: 6g; Cholesterol: 0mg; Sodium: 285mg; Carbohydrates: 25g; Fiber: 1g; Protein: 3g

Salmon Hash

SERVES 6

In the Pacific Northwest, we eat salmon for breakfast, lunch, and dinner. This salmon hash recipe is fashioned after a classic dish you'll find in many restaurants in this area. If you can't find fresh salmon, frozen salmon works beautifully. Serve it with a side of crème fraîche or sour cream, some lemon wedges, and fresh dill. I like to top this dish with a poached egg.

GLUTEN-FREE, NUT-FREE, UNDER 30 MINUTES

PREP TIME: 10 minutes
TOTAL COOK TIME: 15 minutes

AIR CRISP: 8 minutes at 375°F

ACCESSORIES: Cook & Crisp™ basket

VARIATION TIP: This salmon dish is best enjoyed early on during meal prep weeks. Later in the week, combine leftovers with lightly beaten eggs and bake the mixture as a breakfast casserole.

STORAGE: Store in airtight containers in the refrigerator for up to 4 days or in the freezer for up to 3 months.

8 ounces skinless salmon fillets, flaked into small pieces

2 tablespoons sour cream

1 teaspoon Dijon mustard

1 teaspoon prepared horseradish

2 teaspoons chopped fresh dill or dried dill

2 tablespoons extra-virgin olive oil

3 medium russet potatoes

½ cup chopped onion

1 garlic clove, minced

½ teaspoon kosher salt

¼ teaspoon freshly ground black pepper

1. Select SEAR/SAUTÉ on your Ninja® Foodi™ and set the temperature to HI. Select START/STOP to begin. Let preheat for 5 minutes.

2. Meanwhile, in a large bowl, mix together the salmon, sour cream, mustard, horseradish, and dill until well combined. Set aside.

3. Pour the olive oil into the pot. Once the oil is hot, add the potatoes and onion and sauté for 4 to 5 minutes, stirring regularly to evenly cook the potatoes and soften the onion. Add the garlic and sauté for 2 more minutes. Select START/STOP.

4. Using oven mitts, lift the pot out of the Foodi™ and carefully pour the potato mixture into the bowl with the salmon. Return the pot to the Foodi™. Using a wooden spoon, gently toss the ingredients together until the potatoes are evenly coated.

5. Place a piece of parchment paper in the bottom of the Cook & Crisp™ basket. Carefully place the potato-salmon mixture in the basket. Lower the basket into the Foodi™ pot.

6. Close the crisping lid. Select AIR CRISP, set the temperature to 375ºF, and set the time to 8 minutes. Select START/STOP to begin. After 4 minutes, open the lid and stir the hash. Close the lid and continue cooking for 4 additional minutes.

7. When cooking is complete, open the lid and remove the basket. Season with the salt and pepper.

Per serving: *Calories: 192; Total fat: 8g; Saturated fat: 1g; Cholesterol: 23mg; Sodium: 134mg; Carbohydrates: 21g; Fiber: 2g; Protein: 10g*

French Toast Casserole

SERVES 8

This is an incredible meal prep dish that can be enjoyed for breakfast all week long, and it's also a fantastic make-ahead dish to feed a hungry brunch crowd. My daughter likes to call this a "breakfast dessert," and we make it a lot.

NUT-FREE, VEGETARIAN

PREP TIME: 10 minutes
TOTAL COOK TIME:
39 minutes

APPROX. PRESSURE
BUILD: 7 minutes
PRESSURE COOK:
25 minutes
PRESSURE RELEASE:
quick

AIR CRISP: 7 minutes at
325°F

ACCESSORIES: Foodi™
all-purpose pan

PREP TIP: You can skip
the icing completely to
save time (and calories).

STORAGE: Store in an
airtight container in the
refrigerator for up to
4 days or in the freezer
for up to 3 months.

7 tablespoons unsalted butter, at room temperature, divided

1 (14- to 16-ounce) loaf stale brioche, challah, or French bread, cut into 1-inch cubes

6 large eggs

1¼ cups plus 1 tablespoon whole milk

6 tablespoons packed light brown sugar, divided

2½ teaspoons vanilla extract, divided

3 teaspoons cinnamon, divided

¼ teaspoon kosher salt

1 cup water

2 tablespoons cream cheese, at room temperature

1 cup powdered sugar

1 tablespoon whole milk

1. Grease a Foodi™ all-purpose pan with 1 tablespoon of butter. Line the bottom with parchment paper.

2. Place the cubed bread in a large bowl. Set aside.

3. In a medium bowl, whisk together the eggs, milk, 4 tablespoons of brown sugar, 2 teaspoon of vanilla, 2 teaspoons of cinnamon, and ½ teaspoon of salt. Pour the egg mixture over the bread and mix to evenly coat the bread. Gently transfer the bread to the prepared all-purpose pan.

4. In a small microwave-safe bowl, melt 4 tablespoons of butter in the microwave. Add the remaining 2 tablespoons of brown sugar, 1 teaspoon of cinnamon, and salt. Drizzle the topping evenly over the bread. Cover the baking dish with aluminum foil.

5. Pour the water into the inner pot of your Ninja® Foodi™. Place the Deluxe Reversible Rack in the lower steam position without the Deluxe Layer installed and lower the rack into the Foodi™ pot. Place the pan on the rack.

6. Assemble the pressure lid, making sure the pressure release valve is in the SEAL position. Select PRESSURE and set it to HI. Set the time to 25 minutes. Select START/STOP to begin.

7. Meanwhile, make the icing. In a large bowl, whisk together the cream cheese and remaining 2 tablespoons of butter until creamy. Mix in the powdered sugar, milk, and remaining ½ teaspoon of vanilla.

8. When the pressure cooking is complete, quick release the pressure by turning the pressure release valve to the VENT position. Carefully remove the lid when the unit has finished releasing pressure.

9. Remove the foil. Select AIR CRISP, set the temperature to 325°F, and set the time to 7 minutes. Select START/STOP to begin.

10. When cooking is complete, open the crisping lid and remove the pan. Let the casserole cool at room temperature for 5 minutes, then drizzle the icing over the top before serving.

Per serving: Calories: 403; Total fat: 17g; Saturated fat: 9g; Cholesterol: 173mg; Sodium: 466mg; Carbohydrates: 51g; Fiber: 2g; Protein: 11g

Creamy Mexican-Inspired Corn Chowder, *page 132*

4

SOUPS, STEWS, AND CHILIS

Creamy Mexican-Inspired Corn Chowder

SERVES 6

This rich corn chowder is one of my personal favorite recipes. It's on regular rotation at our house, and I hope you'll love it, too. With an abundance of sweet corn, plus aromatic spices and a silky, creamy base, this chowder is the ultimate comfort food. It's versatile, too: Make it vegetarian by omitting the bacon, and/ or make it dairy-free by substituting coconut milk for the half-and-half.

GLUTEN-FREE, NUT-FREE

PREP TIME: 10 minutes
TOTAL COOK TIME: 38 minutes

APPROX. PRESSURE BUILD: 10 minutes
PRESSURE COOK: 5 minutes
PRESSURE RELEASE: natural for 10 minutes, then quick

SAUTÉ: 13 minutes

VARIATION TIP: You may omit the jalapeño if you wish to keep the flavor mild. Or, add more jalapeño and chili powder to bump up the heat.

- 4 slices bacon, cut into small pieces
- 1 tablespoon unsalted butter
- ½ cup finely diced yellow or white onion
- 1 teaspoon finely diced jalapeño, plus additional sliced jalapeño, seeds and veins removed, for garnish (optional)
- 1 teaspoon chili powder
- 1 teaspoon paprika
- 1 teaspoon ground cumin
- 4 garlic cloves, minced
- 4 cups chicken broth
- 2 pounds frozen yellow corn kernels
- 1 teaspoon kosher salt
- 1 cup half-and-half
- ¼ cup cornstarch
- 3 tablespoons freshly squeezed lime juice
- ½ cup chopped fresh cilantro, plus extra for garnish (optional)
- Crumbled cotija cheese, for garnish (optional)

1. Select SEAR/SAUTÉ on your Ninja® Foodi™ and set the temperature to HI. Select START/STOP to begin. Let preheat for 5 minutes.

2. Place the bacon in the pot and sauté, stirring often, for 3 to 4 minutes, until it is cooked to your desired crispness. Transfer the bacon to a paper towel–lined plate and set aside. Pour out some of the fat, leaving about 1 tablespoon of bacon grease in the Foodi™ pot.

3. Add the butter to the pot. As it melts, use a wooden spoon to scrape up any brown bits from the bottom of the pot. Stir in the onion and jalapeño. Sprinkle in the chili powder, paprika, and cumin and sauté for 2 to 3 minutes, stirring to combine. Add the garlic and sauté for 1 more minute, just until the garlic is softened. Select START/STOP. Slowly pour in the chicken broth, scraping up any browned bits from the bottom of the pot. Stir in the corn and salt.

4. Assemble the pressure lid, making sure the pressure release valve is in the SEAL position. Select PRESSURE and set it to HI. Set the time to 5 minutes. Select START/STOP to begin.

5. When the pressure cooking is complete, allow the pressure to naturally release for 10 minutes. After 10 minutes, quick release the remaining pressure by moving the pressure release valve to the VENT position. Carefully remove the lid when the unit has finished releasing pressure.

6. Select SEAR/SAUTÉ and set the temperature to M/HI. Select START/STOP to begin.

7. In a medium bowl, whisk together the half-and-half and cornstarch until the cornstarch is dissolved. Stir the mixture into the soup, then stir in the lime juice and cilantro. Simmer, stirring occasionally, until the soup has thickened, 3 to 5 minutes. Select START/STOP.

8. Top with reserved crispy bacon and any optional toppings, including crumbled cotija cheese, sliced jalapeño, and additional chopped cilantro.

STORAGE: Store in airtight containers in the refrigerator for up to 4 days or in the freezer for up to 3 months. If freezing, place in the container after step 8, since soups with dairy do not tend to freeze well. Add that mixture when you reheat the soup.

Per serving: Calories: 291; Total fat: 11g; Saturated fat: 5g; Cholesterol: 29mg; Sodium: 886mg; Carbohydrates: 46g; Fiber: 5g; Protein: 10g

Turkey Chili

Chili is always a fantastic meal prep dish. This recipe makes so many servings, is easy to pull together, freezes well, and reheats beautifully. Thanks to the Foodi™, you can have a robust, hearty, flavorful chili in just about 45 minutes—instead of the several hours it would take on the stove top. In addition to regular dinners, I love to make this chili for potlucks, meal trains, and game day gatherings.

NUT-FREE

PREP TIME: 10 minutes
TOTAL COOK TIME:
47 minutes

APPROX. PRESSURE BUILD: 10 minutes
PRESSURE COOK:
20 minutes
PRESSURE RELEASE:
natural for 10 minutes, then quick

SAUTÉ: 7 minutes

VARIATION TIP: Serve leftovers over tortilla chips for loaded nachos, over mac and cheese for chili mac, or with scrambled eggs for a hearty breakfast or brunch.

STORAGE: Store in airtight containers in the refrigerator for up to 4 days or in the freezer for up to 3 months.

- 6 slices bacon, cut into small pieces
- 1 red bell pepper, diced
- 1 cup diced yellow onion
- 2 garlic cloves, minced
- 1½ pounds ground turkey
- 3 (14.5-ounce) cans mixed chili beans, black beans, pinto beans, red beans, or a mix, drained and rinsed
- 1 (14.5-ounce) can fire-roasted tomatoes
- 1 (14.5-ounce) can beef stock
- 1 (6-ounce) can tomato paste
- 2 tablespoons Worcestershire sauce
- 2 teaspoons dried oregano
- 2 tablespoons chili powder
- 2 teaspoons ground cumin
- 1 teaspoon smoked paprika
- 2 teaspoons kosher salt
- ½ teaspoon freshly ground black pepper
- Optional Toppings: sour cream, chopped fresh cilantro, sliced scallions, finely chopped jalapeño, shredded cheddar cheese

1. Select SEAR/SAUTÉ on your Ninja® Foodi™ and set the temperature to HI. Select START/STOP to begin. Let preheat for 5 minutes.

2. Place the bacon in the pot and sauté, stirring often, for 3 to 4 minutes, until it is cooked to your desired crispness. Transfer the bacon to a paper towel–lined plate. Set aside. Pour out some of the fat, leaving about 1 tablespoon of bacon grease in the Foodi™ pot.

3. Add the red bell pepper, onion, and garlic to the Foodi™ pot and sauté for 2 to 3 minutes, until the peppers are slightly soft. Add the ground turkey and cook, breaking up the meat with a wooden spoon, until it is browned and combined with the vegetables.

4. Add the beans, tomatoes, stock, tomato paste, Worcestershire sauce, oregano, chili powder, cumin, paprika, salt, black pepper, and half of the cooked bacon. Stir to combine. Select START/STOP.

5. Assemble the pressure lid, making sure the pressure release valve is in the SEAL position. Select PRESSURE and set it to HI. Set the time to 20 minutes. Select START/STOP to begin.

6. When the pressure cooking is complete, allow the pressure to release naturally for 10 minutes. After 10 minutes, quick release the remaining pressure by moving the pressure release valve to the VENT position. Carefully remove the lid when the unit has finished releasing pressure.

7. Serve the chili sprinkled with the remaining bacon, as well as sour cream, cilantro, scallions, jalapeños, and cheddar cheese, if desired.

Per serving: Calories: 271; Total fat: 8g; Saturated fat: 2g; Cholesterol: 52mg; Sodium: 518mg; Carbohydrates: 27g; Fiber: 10g; Protein: 24g

Chicken and Wild Rice Soup

SERVES 6

I just love how this light, healthy soup is still so warm and comforting on a chilly day. It's a hearty soup that can stand on its own as the main course, paired with a salad and a loaf of warm, crusty bread.

DAIRY-FREE, NUT-FREE, READY TO GO

PREP TIME: 10 minutes
TOTAL COOK TIME: 37 minutes

APPROX. PRESSURE BUILD: 10 minutes
PRESSURE COOK: 20 minutes
PRESSURE RELEASE: natural for 5 minutes, then quick

SAUTÉ: 7 minutes

READY TO GO: Prep the chicken, carrots, celery, mushrooms, and onion, and put them in resealable bags. Refrigerate for up to 2 days, until you are ready to cook.

STORAGE: Store in airtight containers in the refrigerator for up to 4 days or in the freezer for up to 3 months.

1 tablespoon extra-virgin olive oil

1 pound boneless, skinless chicken breast, cut into bite-size pieces

1½ cups sliced carrots (about 5 medium carrots)

1 cup chopped celery (about 5 stalks)

2½ cups sliced mushrooms (cremini, shiitake, or white button)

½ cup finely chopped yellow onion

3 garlic cloves, minced

1 cup wild rice

6 cups vegetable or chicken broth

½ teaspoon kosher salt

½ teaspoon fresh thyme leaves

1. Select SEAR/SAUTÉ on your Ninja® Foodi™ and set the temperature to HI. Select START/STOP to begin. Let preheat for 5 minutes.

2. Heat the oil in the pot, then add the chicken and sauté for 2 to 3 minutes, stirring occasionally. Add the carrots, celery, mushrooms, onion, and garlic and sauté for 3 to 4 minutes. Add the wild rice, broth, salt, and thyme.

3. Assemble the pressure lid, making sure the valve is in the SEAL position. Select PRESSURE; set to HI. Set the time to 20 minutes. Select START/STOP to begin.

4. When the cooking is complete, quick release the pressure by turning the valve to the VENT position. Carefully remove the lid when the pressure has released.

Per serving: Calories: 266; Total fat: 4g; Saturated fat: 1g; Cholesterol: 43mg; Sodium: 812mg; Carbohydrates: 37g; Fiber: 4g; Protein: 22g

Wonton Soup

Wonton soup was a must whenever we'd eat at a Chinese restaurant when I was growing up. As I got older, I couldn't believe how easy it was to make at home. I make homemade wontons quite a bit, but for meal prep weeks, frozen wontons save time and money. Frozen mini pork wontons work perfectly in this recipe, but you can also use chicken or vegetarian pot stickers or dumplings instead.

DAIRY-FREE, NUT-FREE, UNDER 30 MINUTES

PREP TIME: 5 minutes
TOTAL COOK TIME: 15 minutes

APPROX. PRESSURE BUILD: 10 minutes
PRESSURE COOK: 5 minutes
PRESSURE RELEASE: quick

ONE AND DONE: Sautéing the ginger and garlic releases more flavor into the soup, but you can skip this step and simply add them to the pot with the broth, then cook starting at step 3.

STORAGE: Store in airtight containers in the refrigerator for up to 4 days or in the freezer for up to 3 months.

1 tablespoon toasted sesame oil

1 (1-inch) piece fresh ginger, thinly sliced

2 garlic cloves, minced

8 cups low-sodium chicken broth

20 frozen mini wontons, pot stickers, or dumplings

1. Select SEAR/SAUTÉ on your Ninja® Foodi™ and set the temperature to HI. Select START/STOP to begin. Let preheat for 5 minutes.

2. Pour the sesame oil into the pot. Once the oil is hot, add the ginger and garlic and sauté, stirring constantly, for about 1 minute, just until the garlic and ginger have softened and are fragrant. Pour in the broth and stir in the wontons. Select START/STOP.

3. Assemble the pressure lid, making sure the pressure release valve is in the SEAL position. Select PRESSURE and set it to HI. Set the time to 5 minutes. Select START/STOP to begin.

4. When the cooking is complete, quick release the pressure by turning the pressure release valve to the VENT position. Carefully remove the lid when the unit has finished releasing pressure.

Per serving: *Calories: 139; Total fat: 7g; Saturated fat: 2g; Cholesterol: 8mg; Sodium: 309mg; Carbohydrates: 11g; Fiber: 1g; Protein: 10g*

Lentil Soup

This is an amazing one-and-done pantry recipe that is especially fantastic when you're low on provisions or lacking cooking motivation (hey, we've all been there). If they are properly stored in a cool, dry pantry or cupboard, dried lentils are good for two to three years, and canned tomatoes will retain their best quality for up to 18 months. You can also use fresh or frozen vegetables in this soup.

DAIRY-FREE, GLUTEN-FREE, NUT-FREE, ONE AND DONE, READY TO GO, VEGAN

PREP TIME: 10 minutes
TOTAL COOK TIME: 25 minutes

APPROX. PRESSURE BUILD: 10 minutes
PRESSURE COOK: 15 minutes
PRESSURE RELEASE: quick

READY TO GO: Prep all the ingredients except the spinach, and place them in a large resealable bag. Refrigerate for up to 2 days.

STORAGE: Store in airtight containers in the refrigerator for up to 4 days or in the freezer for up to 3 months.

1 cup chopped yellow or white onion

1 cup chopped carrots (1 to 2 carrots)

½ cup chopped celery (about 2 stalks)

3 garlic cloves, minced

1½ cups green lentils

1 (14.5-ounce) can diced tomatoes

2 teaspoon dried thyme

1 teaspoon dried basil

1 teaspoon dried oregano

½ teaspoon kosher salt

¼ teaspoon freshly ground black pepper

2 (14.5-ounce) cans vegetable broth (about 4 cups)

4 cups baby spinach

1. Combine the onion, carrots, celery, garlic, lentils, and tomatoes in the inner pot of your Ninja® Foodi™. Season with the thyme, basil, oregano, salt, and pepper, then stir in the broth.

2. Assemble the pressure lid, making sure the pressure release valve is in the SEAL position. Select PRESSURE and set it to HI. Set the time to 15 minutes. Select START/STOP to begin.

3. When the cooking is complete, quick release the pressure by turning the pressure release valve to the VENT position. Carefully remove the lid when the unit has finished releasing pressure.

4. Stir in the spinach until it has wilted.

Per serving: Calories: 218; Total fat: 1g; Saturated fat: 0g; Cholesterol: 3mg; Sodium: 676mg; Carbohydrates: 40g; Fiber: 8g; Protein: 15g

Beef Stew

When my family is craving soul-soothing, warm-up-your-bones food, we make this beef stew. Searing the beef locks in flavor, but if you're short on time, you can skip that step and make this a one-and-done recipe by putting all the ingredients except the peas in the Foodi™ and selecting PRESSURE. Also, see the Ready to Go tip for how to make this even easier for meal planning.

DAIRY-FREE, GLUTEN-FREE, NUT-FREE, READY TO GO

PREP TIME: 10 minutes
TOTAL COOK TIME: 40 minutes

APPROX. PRESSURE BUILD: 10 minutes
PRESSURE COOK: 20 minutes
PRESSURE RELEASE: natural for 10 minutes, then quick

- **1½ pounds boneless beef chuck roast, cut into 2-inch pieces**
- **½ teaspoon kosher salt**
- **¼ teaspoon freshly ground black pepper**
- **2 tablespoons extra-virgin olive oil**
- **½ cup diced yellow onion**
- **2 garlic cloves, minced**
- **1 tablespoon tomato paste**
- **1 teaspoon fresh thyme leaves or ½ teaspoon dried thyme**
- **1 (14.5-ounce) can beef broth**
- **2 tablespoons Worcestershire sauce**
- **2 large carrots, cut into 2-inch pieces**
- **2 medium russet potatoes, peeled and cut into 2-inch pieces**
- **1 tablespoon cornstarch**
- **¾ cup frozen peas**

1. Season the beef on all sides with the salt and pepper.

2. Select SEAR/SAUTÉ on your Ninja® Foodi™ and set the temperature to HI. Select START/STOP to begin. Let preheat for 5 minutes.

3. Pour the olive oil into the pot and let it heat for about 1 minute. Add the beef and cook for 3 to 4 minutes, browning the meat on all sides.

4. Add the onion, garlic, tomato paste, and thyme. Sauté for 2 minutes, just until the onion and garlic are soft and fragrant, then pour in the beef broth and Worcestershire sauce and stir to combine. Using a wooden spoon, scrape up any browned bits from the bottom of the pot.

5. Add the carrots and potatoes. Sprinkle the cornstarch over the ingredients and gently stir, mixing in the cornstarch until it has fully dissolved.

6. Assemble the pressure lid, making sure the pressure release valve is in the SEAL position. Select PRESSURE and set it to HI. Set the time to 20 minutes. Select START/ STOP to begin.

7. When the cooking is complete, allow the pressure to naturally release for 10 minutes. After 10 minutes, quick release the remaining pressure by moving the pressure release valve to the VENT position. Carefully remove the lid when the unit has finished releasing pressure.

8. Add the peas to the pot and gently stir until the peas have thawed.

Per serving: Calories: 293; Total fat: 11g; Saturated fat: 3g; Cholesterol: 85mg; Sodium: 570mg; Carbohydrates: 22g; Fiber: 3g; Protein: 27g

READY TO GO: Prep all the ingredients except for the peas ahead of time and place them in a large resealable bag. Refrigerate for up to 2 days or freeze for up to 1 month. When you are ready to cook, bring the ingredients to room temperature for 10 minutes, then place the ingredients in the inner pot and begin cooking at step 7. If cooking from frozen, expect the Foodi™ to take a few more minutes to come to pressure.

STORAGE: Store in airtight containers in the refrigerator for up to 4 days or in the freezer for up to 3 months.

Lasagna Soup

One of my favorite ways to get creative in the kitchen is combining two favorite foods into one—like Cheeseburger Pasta (page 182) and this Lasagna Soup. It's perfect for those days when you want the comfort of a warm bowl of tomato soup and the heartiness of lasagna. This recipe calls for ground turkey, but you can use ground beef, ground chicken, or chopped mushrooms instead.

DAIRY-FREE, NUT-FREE

PREP TIME: 10 minutes
TOTAL COOK TIME:
29 minutes

**APPROX. PRESSURE
BUILD:** 10 minutes
PRESSURE COOK:
6 minutes
PRESSURE RELEASE:
natural for 5 minutes, then quick

SAUTÉ: 8 minutes

PREP TIP: Make this on a meal prep week when you are making other recipes that begin with a mirepoix of carrots, onion, and celery, such as Beef Ragù with Spaghetti (page 44).

- 2 tablespoons extra-virgin olive oil
- 1 pound ground turkey
- 1 cup chopped onion
- 2 garlic cloves, minced
- 1 cup chopped carrots
- 1 cup chopped celery
- 1 cup chopped spinach
- 2 (14.5-ounce) cans beef broth
- 1 (14.5-ounce) can diced tomatoes
- 1 (6-ounce) can tomato paste
- 2 teaspoons dried basil
- 1 bay leaf
- 8 ounces lasagna noodles (about 10), broken into bite-size pieces
- ½ teaspoon kosher salt
- ¼ teaspoon freshly ground black pepper

1. Select SEAR/SAUTÉ on your Ninja® Foodi™ and set the temperature to HI. Select START/STOP to begin. Let preheat for 5 minutes.

2. Pour the olive oil into the Foodi™ pot. Once the oil is hot, add the turkey and cook for 3 to 4 minutes, using a wooden spoon to break the meat into smaller pieces, until the meat is evenly browned. Add the onion, garlic, carrots, celery, and spinach. Sauté until the vegetables are slightly softened, 3 to 4 minutes. Select START/STOP.

3. Add the beef broth to the pot, then use a wooden spoon to gently scrape up any browned bits from the bottom of the pot. Add the diced tomatoes and stir in the tomato paste. Sprinkle in the basil and add the bay leaf.

4. Lay the lasagna noodles on top of the soup, and gently push them down with a wooden spoon so most of the noodle pieces are submerged in the liquid.

5. Assemble the pressure lid, making sure the pressure release valve is in the SEAL position. Select PRESSURE and set it to HI. Set the time to 6 minutes. Select START/STOP to begin.

6. When the cooking is complete, allow the pressure to release naturally for 5 minutes. After 5 minutes, quick release remaining pressure by moving the pressure release valve to the VENT position. Carefully remove the lid when the unit has finished releasing pressure.

7. Open lid and stir the soup. Season with the salt and pepper before serving or storing.

Per serving: Calories: 360; Total fat: 12g; Saturated fat: 2g; Cholesterol: 55mg; Sodium: 830mg; Carbohydrates: 42g; Fiber: 5g; Protein: 23g

VARIATION TIP: For a creamier, cheesy lasagna soup, after pressure cooking is complete, stir in some heavy (whipping) cream and a combination of cheeses, such as Parmesan cheese, mozzarella cheese, and/or ricotta cheese.

STORAGE: Store in airtight containers in the refrigerator for up to 4 days or in the freezer for up to 3 months.

Mushroom Soup

Mushroom soup is elegant enough to serve at dinner parties, yet super simple and fast enough to make any day of the week. It's also highly versatile, which can result in creative leftovers. With some cornstarch or arrowroot powder, you can thicken it up to the consistency of gravy and serve it over poultry or mashed potatoes, or even use it as a sauce for pasta.

DAIRY-FREE, GLUTEN-FREE, NUT-FREE, READY TO GO, VEGAN

PREP TIME: 10 minutes
TOTAL COOK TIME: 23 minutes

APPROX. PRESSURE BUILD: 10 minutes
PRESSURE COOK: 5 minutes
PRESSURE RELEASE: quick

SAUTÉ: 8 minutes

VARIATION TIP: For creamier, thicker soup, after the pressure cooking is complete, ladle 2 cups of soup into a high-powered blender along with 2 teaspoons of cornstarch. Blend until smooth. Pour the blended mixture back into the pot with the rest of the soup and stir to combine.

- 2 tablespoons extra-virgin olive oil
- ½ cup finely chopped yellow onion
- 1 pound cremini, shiitake, or white button mushrooms, sliced
- 3 garlic cloves, minced
- ½ tablespoon fresh thyme leaves or 1 teaspoon dried thyme
- 1½ teaspoon kosher salt
- 1 teaspoon freshly ground black pepper
- 3 cups vegetable broth
- 1 cup full-fat coconut milk

1. Select SEAR/SAUTÉ on your Ninja® Foodi™ and set the temperature to HI. Select START/STOP to begin. Let preheat for 5 minutes.

2. Pour the olive oil into the pot. Once the oil is hot, add the onion and sauté for 2 to 3 minutes, stirring often until softened. Add the mushrooms, garlic, thyme, salt, and pepper and sauté for 4 to 5 more minutes, until the mushrooms are browned evenly and the garlic is soft and fragrant. Select START/STOP. Pour in the broth and coconut milk and stir to combine.

3. Assemble the pressure lid, making sure the pressure release valve is in the SEAL position. Select PRESSURE and set it to HI. Set the time to 5 minutes. Select START/STOP to begin.

4. When the cooking is complete, quick release the pressure by turning the pressure release valve to the VENT position. Carefully remove the lid when the unit has finished releasing pressure.

Per serving: Calories: 153; Total fat: 13g; Saturated fat: 8g; Cholesterol: 0mg; Sodium: 821mg; Carbohydrates: 9g; Fiber: 2g; Protein: 3g

STORAGE: Store in airtight containers in the refrigerator for up to 4 days or in the freezer for up to 2 months.

Teriyaki Turkey Meatballs with Hoisin-Soy Glaze, *page 156*

5

POULTRY AND SEAFOOD MAINS

Filipino-Style Chicken Adobo

This is a family recipe inspired by the chicken adobo my mother and great-grandmother would make on a regular basis. Every Filipino family has their own distinctive recipe that's slightly different than others. If you've never had this dish before, try it and you'll see why it's immensely popular in restaurants and on dinner tables around the world. Serve chicken adobo over rice or noodles with a side of your favorite vegetables.

DAIRY-FREE, NUT-FREE

PREP TIME: 5 minutes
TOTAL COOK TIME:
37 minutes

APPROX. PRESSURE
BUILD: 10 minutes
PRESSURE COOK:
9 minutes
PRESSURE RELEASE:
quick

SAUTÉ: 18 minutes

STORAGE: Store in airtight containers in the refrigerator for up to 4 days or in the freezer for up to 3 months.

2 pounds bone-in, skin-on chicken thighs and drumsticks

½ tablespoon paprika

1 teaspoon kosher salt

1 teaspoon freshly ground black pepper, divided

2 tablespoons extra-virgin olive oil

¾ cup soy sauce

¼ cup granulated sugar

¾ cup chicken broth

½ cup distilled white vinegar

4 to 5 garlic cloves, minced

1 medium yellow onion, sliced

1 bay leaf

2 scallions, thinly sliced

1. Place the chicken on a plate, pat it dry with paper towels, and season it all over with the paprika, salt, and ½ teaspoon of black pepper.

2. Select SEAR/SAUTÉ on your Ninja® Foodi™ and set the temperature to HI. Select START/STOP to begin. Let preheat for 5 minutes.

3. Pour the olive oil into the pot. Once the oil is hot, add the chicken and cook for 6 to 8 minutes, working in batches if necessary, until it is browned on all sides.

4. Once the chicken pieces are browned evenly, stir in the soy sauce, sugar, chicken broth, vinegar, garlic, onion, bay leaf, and remaining ½ teaspoon of black pepper.

5. Assemble the pressure lid, making sure the pressure release valve is in the SEAL position. Select PRESSURE and set it to HI. Set the time to 9 minutes. Select START/STOP to begin.

6. When the cooking is complete, quick release the pressure by turning the pressure release valve to the VENT position. Carefully remove the lid when the unit has finished releasing pressure.

7. Select SEAR/SAUTÉ and set the temperature to HI. Select START/STOP to begin.

8. Bring the sauce to a boil, then allow it to reduce until it turns dark brown, about 10 minutes.

9. Once the sauce is reduced to your liking, remove the bay leaf. Select START/STOP. Garnish with the scallions before serving.

Per serving: Calories: 351; Total fat: 23g; Saturated fat: 6g; Cholesterol: 111mg; Sodium: 1435mg; Carbohydrates: 12g; Fiber: 1g; Protein: 22g

Crispy Paprika Chicken

Get ready to enjoy flavorful, crispy, juicy chicken in under 30 minutes! I make this for my family often. We eat it when we're craving fried chicken but want a lighter version. Flipping the chicken halfway through cooking ensures even crisping. This is a great meal prep dish because it can be served so many ways: It's delicious with pasta, rice, mashed potatoes, quinoa, fries, tots, or mixed greens.

DAIRY-FREE, GLUTEN-FREE, NUT-FREE, UNDER 30 MINUTES

PREP TIME: 5 minutes
TOTAL COOK TIME: 20 minutes

AIR CRISP: 20 minutes at 375°F

ACCESSORIES: Deluxe Reversible Rack

PREP TIP: You can prepare the dry rub and coat the chicken with it, then refrigerate for up to 1 day in advance. When ready to cook, continue with step 4 of the instructions.

2 garlic cloves, minced

3 teaspoons paprika

1 teaspoon dried oregano

½ teaspoon onion powder

½ teaspoon kosher salt

¼ teaspoon freshly ground black pepper

2 pounds bone-in, skin-on chicken thighs

Nonstick cooking spray

1. Close the crisping lid of your Ninja® Foodi™. Select AIR CRISP and set the temperature to 375°F. Select START/STOP to begin. Let preheat for 5 minutes.

2. Meanwhile, in a small bowl, mix together the garlic, paprika, oregano, onion powder, salt, and pepper.

3. Place the chicken thighs in a large resealable bag, pour in the garlic-spice mixture, and seal the bag. Toss until the chicken is evenly coated.

4. Spray the Deluxe Reversible Rack with cooking spray, then place it in the lower steam position without the Deluxe Layer installed. Place half of the chicken onto the rack and lower the rack into the Foodi™ pot. Next, install the Deluxe Layer on the rack and place the remaining chicken on it.

5. Close the crisping lid. Select AIR CRISP, set the temperature to 375°F, and set the time to 20 minutes. Select START/STOP to begin.

6. After 10 minutes, open the lid and carefully remove the rack. Flip the chicken thighs and, return the rack to the pot. Close the lid and continue cooking for the remaining 10 minutes.

7. Cooking is complete when the chicken is crispy and the internal temperature reads at least 165°F on a food thermometer. Remove the rack from the Foodi™ and serve.

Per serving: *Calories: 256; Total fat: 19g; Saturated fat: 5g; Cholesterol: 111mg; Sodium: 190mg; Carbohydrates: 2g; Fiber: 1g; Protein: 19g*

STORAGE: Store in airtight containers in the refrigerator for up to 4 days or in the freezer for up to 3 months. To reheat, place in the Cook & Crisp™ basket, and air crisp at 350°F in 2-minute increments.

Chicken Fettuccine Alfredo

SERVES 6

Invented by Alfredo di Lelio in 1914, fettuccine Alfredo—originally a simple pasta dish with butter and Parmesan cheese—never really became as popular in Italy as it has in the United States. Two actors tasted Alfredo's recipe while filming in Rome, asked him for the recipe, and brought it back to the United States, where it became popular among the Hollywood elite. Now a classic family favorite, my version of this recipe includes mushrooms for added flavor and texture.

NUT-FREE

PREP TIME: 5 minutes
TOTAL COOK TIME:
28 minutes

APPROX. PRESSURE BUILD: 10 minutes
PRESSURE COOK:
6 minutes
PRESSURE RELEASE:
quick

SAUTÉ: 12 minutes

VARIATION TIP: You can make this recipe without the mushrooms. Try substituting broccoli, spinach, or frozen peas with a squeeze of lemon juice, or substituting shrimp for the chicken.

1½ **pounds boneless, skinless chicken thighs, cut into 1-inch pieces**

½ **teaspoon kosher salt**

¼ **teaspoon freshly ground black pepper**

2 **tablespoons extra-virgin olive oil**

4 **ounces cremini or white button mushrooms, sliced**

3 **garlic cloves, minced**

¼ **cup dry white wine**

3 **cups chicken stock**

12 **ounces fettuccine pasta**

1 **cup heavy (whipping) cream**

½ **cup grated Parmesan cheese**

2 **tablespoons chopped fresh parsley**

1. Pat the chicken dry with paper towels, then season with the salt and pepper.

2. Select SEAR/SAUTÉ on your Ninja® Foodi™ and set the temperature to HI. Select START/STOP to begin. Let preheat for 5 minutes.

3. Pour the olive oil into the pot. Once the oil is hot, add the mushrooms and sauté for 2 to 3 minutes, just until softened. Transfer to a plate and set aside.

4. Add the chicken to the Foodi™ pot and sauté for 3 to 4 minutes, just until browned on all sides. Add the garlic and sauté for 1 more minute. Select START/STOP.

5. Pour in the wine and use a wooden spoon to scrape up any browned bits at the bottom of the pot. Pour in the chicken stock, then place the noodles in the pot in crisscross layers, breaking them in half if necessary to fit. Gently push the noodles down to submerge them in the liquid.

6. Assemble the pressure lid, making sure the pressure release valve is in the SEAL position. Select PRESSURE and set it to HI. Set the time to 6 minutes. Select START/STOP to begin.

7. When the cooking is complete, quick release the pressure by turning the pressure release valve to the VENT position. Carefully remove the lid when the unit has finished releasing pressure.

8. Select SEAR/SAUTÉ and set the heat to MD:HI. Select START/STOP to begin.

9. Stir in the heavy cream and Parmesan, then the mushrooms. Continue stirring and cooking for about 5 minutes, until the sauce has thickened. Serve garnished with the parsley.

Per serving: Calories: 582; Total fat: 27g; Saturated fat: 12g; Cholesterol: 171mg; Sodium: 838mg; Carbohydrates: 47g; Fiber: 2g; Protein: 34g

STORAGE: Store in airtight containers in the refrigerator for up to 4 days or in the freezer for up to 2 months. To reheat in the Foodi™, select SEAR/SAUTÉ and set the temperature to MD:HI. Select START/STOP to begin. Transfer your leftover portion to the Foodi™ pot, along with 1 tablespoon of water, and stir until the pasta is heated through. Add more water as needed to soften the noodles and add creaminess to the sauce as it reheats. To reheat refrigerated pasta in the microwave, place a serving into a microwave-safe bowl with 1 to 2 teaspoons of water or cream. The extra liquid adds some creaminess to the sauce that may have been lost during refrigeration. Microwave in 45-second increments until hot.

Crispy Chicken Wings

SERVES 6

Whether we're gearing up for a gathering or making dinner on another busy weeknight, these crispy chicken wings are always a favorite among friends and family. Thanks to the Foodi™, even a super simple recipe shines; this one has only a few ingredients, and the wings come out extra crispy without being fried. Serve these with your favorite dipping sauce, or enjoy them as they are with a side of fries, tots, or a veggie platter.

DAIRY-FREE, NUT-FREE, UNDER 30 MINUTES

PREP TIME: 5 minutes
TOTAL COOK TIME: 24 minutes

AIR CRISP: 12 minutes at 380°F + 12 minutes at 400°F

ACCESSORIES: Deluxe Reversible Rack

VARIATION TIP: Make these gluten-free by substituting arrowroot starch powder for the all-purpose flour.

Nonstick cooking spray

3 pounds chicken wings, split into flats and drums

3 tablespoons all-purpose flour

½ teaspoon kosher salt

¼ teaspoon freshly ground black pepper

1. Close the crisping lid of your Ninja® Foodi™. Select AIR CRISP and set the temperature to 375°F. Select START/STOP to begin. Let preheat for 5 minutes.

2. Spray the Deluxe Reversible Rack with cooking spray.

3. Pat all sides of the chicken wings dry with a paper towel, then place the chicken in a large bowl. Sprinkle the flour, salt, and pepper over the chicken, then use your hands to lightly and evenly coat the wings. Place the Deluxe Reversible Rack in the lower steam position without the Deluxe Layer installed and place half of the chicken on the rack. Next, install the Deluxe Layer on the rack and place the remaining chicken on it. Open the crisping lid, and carefully lower the rack into the pot.

4. Close the crisping lid. Select AIR CRISP, set the temperature to 380°F, and set the time to 12 minutes. Select START/STOP to begin.

5. After 12 minutes, carefully lift the rack out of the pot. Use tongs to move the wings on the bottom rack to the top and vice versa, and then flip the wings. Return the rack to the pot. Close the crisping lid. Select AIR CRISP, set the temperature to 400ºF, and set the time to 12 minutes. Select START/STOP to begin.

6. Cooking is complete when the internal temperature of the chicken reads at least 165ºF on a food thermometer. When cooking is complete, open the lid and remove the racks from the Foodi™.

Per serving: Calories: 514; Total fat: 36g; Saturated fat: 10g; Cholesterol: 170mg; Sodium: 257mg; Carbohydrates: 3g; Fiber: g; Protein: 42g

STORAGE: Store in airtight containers in the refrigerator for up to 4 days or in the freezer for up to 3 months. To reheat, place the wings in the Cook & Crisp™ basket and lower the basket into the Foodi™ pot. Close the crisping lid, select AIR CRISP, set the temperature to 350°F, and set the time to 2 minutes.

Teriyaki Turkey Meatballs with Hoisin-Soy Glaze

SERVES 6

These meatballs are wonderfully versatile, making them a meal prep favorite. You can make the meatballs and refrigerate them the night before meal prep day. Once they are cooked, enjoy them over rice, couscous, or quinoa. Serve leftovers in hoagie rolls with cabbage slaw or over rice noodles.

DAIRY-FREE, NUT-FREE

PREP TIME: 10 minutes
TOTAL COOK TIME:
29 minutes

APPROX. PRESSURE
BUILD: 10 minutes
PRESSURE COOK:
15 minutes
PRESSURE RELEASE:
quick

SAUTÉ: 4 minutes

READY TO GO: You can make the meatballs (step 1) and the sauce (step 3) one day ahead of time and store them in separate airtight containers in the refrigerator. When you are ready to cook, let the meatballs and sauce sit at room temperature for about 5 minutes, then resume the instructions starting at step 4.

1½ pounds ground turkey

3 garlic cloves, minced

1 teaspoon minced
  fresh ginger

4 tablespoons soy
  sauce, divided

1 scallion, green parts
  only, chopped

½ cup panko bread crumbs

1 large egg, lightly beaten

2 tablespoons hoisin sauce

1 tablespoon rice vinegar

½ tablespoon packed
  light brown sugar

1 teaspoon toasted
  sesame oil

¾ cup water

1. In a large bowl, mix together the ground turkey, garlic, ginger, 2 tablespoons of soy sauce, scallion, panko bread crumbs, and egg. Form the mixture into 1½-inch meatballs (about 36 to 40 meatballs). Place the meatballs on a plate; cover and refrigerate while you make the sauce.

2. Select SEAR/SAUTÉ on your Ninja® Foodi™ and set the temperature to HI. Select START/STOP to begin. Let preheat for 5 minutes.

3. Meanwhile, in a medium bowl, combine the remaining 2 tablespoons of soy sauce, hoisin sauce, rice vinegar, and brown sugar. Whisk until the sugar is dissolved. Set aside.

4. Pour the sesame oil into the pot. Once the oil is hot, add the meatballs and cook for 3 to 4 minutes, until the meatballs have browned on all sides. Select START/STOP. Transfer the meatballs to a bowl and set aside.

5. Pour the water into the pot, and use a wooden spoon to scrape up any browned bits from the bottom of the pot. Pour in half of the prepared sauce, then return the meatballs to the pot.

6. Assemble the pressure lid, making sure the pressure release valve is in the SEAL position. Select PRESSURE and set it to HI. Set the time to 15 minutes. Select START/ STOP to begin.

7. When the cooking is complete, quick release the pressure by turning the pressure release valve to the VENT position. Carefully remove the lid when the unit has finished releasing pressure.

8. Pour the remaining sauce into the pot, and stir to coat the meatballs.

STORAGE: Store in airtight containers in the refrigerator for up to 4 days or in the freezer for up to 3 months.

Per serving: *Calories: 232; Total fat: 11g; Saturated fat: 3g; Cholesterol: 109mg; Sodium: 540mg; Carbohydrates: 9g; Fiber: 1g; Protein: 25g*

Fiesta Chicken and Black Beans

SERVES 6

This fiesta chicken is a family-friendly dish that comes together quickly, thanks to the Foodi™ and easy pantry staples like store-bought taco seasoning and salsa. Serve it simply over rice, pile it on top of tortilla chips for loaded nachos, or use it as a chicken taco filling. You can warm up leftovers with scrambled eggs and top with sour cream and avocados for a hearty breakfast.

DAIRY-FREE, NUT-FREE, ONE AND DONE

PREP TIME: 5 minutes
TOTAL COOK TIME: 30 minutes

APPROX. PRESSURE BUILD: 10 minutes
PRESSURE COOK: 20 minutes
PRESSURE RELEASE: quick

STORAGE: Store in airtight containers in the refrigerator for up to 4 days or in the freezer for up to 2 months.

2 pounds boneless, skinless chicken thighs

¼ cup taco seasoning

2 (14.5-ounce) cans black beans, drained and rinsed

1½ cups corn, fresh or frozen (no need to thaw)

1½ cups salsa

1 cup chicken broth

1. In a large bowl, combine the chicken and taco seasoning; toss gently to coat the meat evenly on all sides.

2. Place the chicken, beans, and corn in the inner pot of your Ninja® Foodi™ and stir to combine. Top with the salsa. Pour in the chicken broth, and gently push down to submerge the ingredients in the liquid.

3. Assemble the pressure lid, making sure the pressure release valve is in the SEAL position. Select PRESSURE and set it to HI. Set the time to 20 minutes. Select START/STOP to begin.

4. When the cooking is complete, quick release the pressure by turning the pressure release valve to the VENT position. Carefully remove the lid when the unit has finished releasing pressure.

5. Transfer the chicken to a large bowl. Shred the meat using two forks, then stir it into the black beans in the pot.

Per serving: *Calories: 369; Total fat: 7g; Saturated fat: 2g; Cholesterol: 143mg; Sodium: 934mg; Carbohydrates: 36g; Fiber: 10g; Protein: 40g*

Beer-Battered Fish

Double-dipping the fish—first in a wet batter, then in a dry coat of seasoned flour—and then allowing the fish to chill before crisping locks in the batter, making it less likely to drip off the fish while it's crisping. This results in that delicious, crispy crunch you expect from beer-battered fish—without lots of oil. After enjoying this with fries for classic fish and chips, make fish sandwiches with leftovers.

DAIRY-FREE, NUT-FREE

PREP TIME: 15 minutes, plus 10 minutes to chill
TOTAL COOK TIME: 10 minutes

AIR CRISP: 10 minutes at 400°F

ACCESSORIES: Cook & Crisp™ basket

PREP TIP: For the batter, use a beer that you enjoy drinking, since the fish will soak up that flavor. Lighter beers, such as a lager, IPA, pale ale, or pilsner, work best.

- 3 cups all-purpose flour, divided
- 2 teaspoons baking powder
- ½ teaspoon kosher salt
- ¼ teaspoon freshly ground black pepper
- 1 (12-ounce) bottle light beer, such as lager or pale ale
- 1 large egg, lightly beaten
- 1 teaspoon Old Bay seasoning
- 3 pounds skinless, boneless, large-flake whitefish fillets, such as cod, hake, or halibut
- Nonstick cooking spray
- Malt vinegar and tartar sauce, for serving (optional)

1. Cover one-quarter of a baking sheet or large plate with parchment paper. Set aside.

2. Set out two large bowls. In the first bowl, whisk together 1½ cups of flour and the baking powder, salt, pepper, beer, and egg until relatively smooth. There should be no large chunks of flour or baking powder.

3. In the second bowl, mix the remaining 1½ cups flour with the Old Bay seasoning.

4. Pat the fish fillets dry with paper towels. Working with one fillet at a time, dip the fish into the wet batter, allowing the batter to coat all sides. Gently shake off any excess batter, then immediately dredge the fish into the dry flour mixture. Place the coated fillet on the prepared baking sheet.

CONTINUED ▶

Beer-Battered Fish continued

5. Repeat the dredging process with the remaining fillets, then refrigerate the coated fillets for 10 minutes to allow them to chill and set.

6. Select SEAR/SAUTÉ on your Ninja® Foodi™ and set the temperature to HI. Select START/STOP to begin. Let preheat for 5 minutes.

7. Spray the inside of the Cook & Crisp™ basket with cooking spray and place it in the Foodi™ pot. Place the coated fish fillets in the basket in a single layer. You may need to work in batches if your fish won't fit in one layer. Spray the tops of fillets lightly with cooking spray.

8. Close the crisping lid. Select AIR CRISP, set the temperature to 400°F, and set the time to 10 minutes. Select START/STOP to begin.

9. When the cooking is complete, carefully lift the basket out of the Foodi™ pot and transfer the fish onto a clean plate. Repeat steps 7 and 8 if you need to cook a second batch. Serve with malt vinegar and tartar sauce (if using).

Per serving: Calories: 350; Total fat: 4g; Saturated fat: 1g; Cholesterol: 142mg; Sodium: 363mg; Carbohydrates: 26g; Fiber: 1g; Protein: 47g

Shrimp Scampi with Linguine

SERVES 6

Restaurant-quality shrimp scampi with linguine is easy to make at home. When I lived in Boston, I'd splurge on shrimp scampi at any one of the amazing Italian restaurants in the North End. If only I had known then how easy and inexpensive it is to make from scratch. The Foodi™ makes it possible to cook al dente pasta, succulent shrimp, and a light garlic-wine sauce together in one pot in under 20 minutes.

NUT-FREE, UNDER 30 MINUTES

PREP TIME: 5 minutes
TOTAL COOK TIME: 19 minutes

APPROX. PRESSURE BUILD: 10 minutes
PRESSURE COOK: 5 minutes
PRESSURE RELEASE: quick

SAUTÉ: 4 minutes

VARIATION TIP: Shallots are used in traditional shrimp scampi recipes because they offer a milder flavor than onions do. However, if you are meal prepping with other dishes that use onions, feel free to use a small yellow or white onion instead of the shallot.

- 2 tablespoons unsalted butter
- 1 shallot, minced
- 4 garlic cloves, minced
- ½ cup dry white wine
- 12 ounces linguine (or fettuccine) pasta
- 3 cups seafood stock or water
- ½ teaspoon kosher salt
- ¼ teaspoon freshly ground black pepper
- 1 pound frozen large shrimp (between 30 and 40 shrimp)
- 1 tablespoon freshly squeezed lemon juice
- 1 tablespoon chopped fresh basil
- ½ cup grated Parmesan cheese
- 1 tablespoon chopped fresh parsley (optional)

1. Select SEAR/SAUTÉ on your Ninja® Foodi™ and set the temperature to MD:HI. Select START/STOP to begin. Let preheat for 5 minutes.

2. Place the butter in the pot. Once the butter is completely melted, add the shallot and garlic and sauté, stirring often, for 1 minute. Add the wine to the pot, using a wooden spoon to scrape up any browned bits from the bottom of the pot. Cook until reduced, about 1 minute. Select START/STOP.

3. Break the linguine in half, and place it in crisscross layers in the pot. Pour in the seafood stock and season with the salt and black pepper. Gently nudge the noodles to submerge them in the liquid as much as possible.

4. Assemble the pressure lid, making sure the pressure release valve is in the SEAL position. Select PRESSURE and set it to HI. Set the time to 5 minutes. Select START/STOP to begin.

5. When the cooking is complete, quick release the pressure by moving the pressure release valve to the VENT position. Carefully remove the lid when the unit has finished releasing pressure.

6. Select SEAR/SAUTÉ and set the temperature to MD:HI. Select START/STOP to begin. Add the shrimp to the pot, and gently stir it into the pasta. The shrimp will cook in 2 to 4 minutes. When the shrimp has turned pink and is fully cooked, drizzle the lemon juice over the pasta and sprinkle in the basil and Parmesan cheese. Select START/STOP.

7. Plate the pasta and garnish with parsley, if using.

Per serving: Calories: 354; Total fat: 8g; Saturated fat: 4g; Cholesterol: 113mg; Sodium: 681mg; Carbohydrates: 46g; Fiber: 2g; Protein: 20g

STORAGE: Store in airtight containers in the refrigerator for up to 2 to 3 days. This dish is best enjoyed earlier in your meal prep week. To reheat in the Foodi™, select SEAR/SAUTÉ and set the temperature to MD:HI. Select START/STOP to begin. Transfer your leftover portion to the Foodi™ pot, along with 1 tablespoon of water, and stir until it is heated through. Add more water as needed to soften the noodles and add creaminess to the sauce as it reheats. To reheat in the microwave, add 1 tablespoon of water or extra-virgin olive oil to individual servings and reheat in 1-minute increments until heated through.

Seafood Jambalaya

Whenever I make this, I'm transported back to New Orleans. This flavorful dish starts with what's known as "the holy trinity" in Creole and Cajun cooking—onion, bell pepper, and celery—which are sautéed with spices. The shrimp soaks up all of the delicious flavors, and the andouille sausage adds a nice kick. This is soul-soothing Southern comfort food that freezes and reheats well, making it ideal for meal planning.

DAIRY-FREE, GLUTEN-FREE, NUT-FREE

PREP TIME: 10 minutes
TOTAL COOK TIME: 36 minutes

APPROX. PRESSURE BUILD: 10 minutes
PRESSURE COOK: 5 minutes
PRESSURE RELEASE: natural for 5 minutes, then quick

SAUTÉ: 16 minutes

VARIATION TIP: To make this mild, substitute your favorite mild sausage or bratwurst for the andouille sausage, use regular paprika instead of smoked paprika, and leave out the cayenne pepper.

- 2 tablespoons extra-virgin olive oil
- 12 ounces andouille sausage, cut into ½-inch thick slices
- ½ cup diced yellow or white onion
- 1 red bell pepper, chopped
- ½ cup chopped celery
- 3 garlic cloves, minced
- 1 teaspoon smoked paprika
- ½ teaspoon dried oregano
- ½ teaspoon cayenne pepper
- 2 cups chicken broth, divided
- 1½ cups long-grain white rice, rinsed and drained
- 1 (14.5-ounce) can diced tomatoes
- ½ teaspoon kosher salt
- ¼ teaspoon freshly ground black pepper
- 3 cups large shrimp, peeled, tails removed (about 22 to 24 shrimp)
- ½ cup peas

1. Select SEAR/SAUTÉ on your Ninja® Foodi™ and set the temperature to HI. Select START/STOP to begin. Let preheat for 5 minutes.

2. Pour the olive oil into the pot. Once the oil is hot, add the sausage and sear it evenly on both sides, about 1 to 2 minutes per side. Transfer the sausage to a paper towel–lined plate to drain.

3. Add the onion, bell pepper, celery, garlic, paprika, oregano, and cayenne pepper to the Foodi™ pot. Sauté for 2 minutes, just until vegetables are soft and fragrant. Add a tablespoon or so of chicken broth to the pot, then use a wooden spoon to scrape up the browned bits from the bottom of the pot. Select START/STOP. Stir in the rice, tomatoes, salt, and pepper.

4. Pour in the remaining chicken broth, and gently press down on the rice and vegetable mixture to submerge it in the liquid.

5. Assemble the pressure lid, making sure the pressure release valve is in the SEAL position. Select PRESSURE and set it to HI. Set the time to 5 minutes. Select START/STOP to begin.

6. When the cooking is complete, allow the pressure to release naturally for 5 minutes. After 5 minutes, quick release the remaining pressure by moving the pressure release valve to the VENT position. Carefully remove the lid when the unit has finished releasing pressure.

7. Stir the ingredients in the pot. Add the sausage, shrimp, and peas. Gently push the shrimp down a bit so it's mostly covered by the rice.

8. Reassemble the pressure lid. Allow the shrimp to cook in the residual heat until they are fully cooked, about 5 or 10 minutes. When the shrimp has turned pink and is cooked through, give the jambalaya a good stir before serving.

STORAGE: Store in airtight containers in the refrigerator for up to 4 days or in the freezer for up to 3 months. To reheat in the Foodi™, select SEAR/SAUTÉ and set the temperature to MD:HI. Select START/STOP to begin. Transfer your leftover portion to the Foodi™ pot, along with 1 tablespoon of water, and stir until it is heated through. Add more water as needed to soften the rice as it reheats. To reheat in the microwave, add 1 tablespoon of water to each individual serving, and reheat in 1-minute increments until hot.

Per serving: Calories: 543; Total fat: 21g; Saturated fat: 6g; Cholesterol: 217mg; Sodium: 915mg; Carbohydrates: 47g; Fiber: 4g; Protein: 39g

Salmon Patties

Salmon patties are a tasty, versatile addition to any meal planning menu. Serve them with a side salad, make a salmon cake sandwich for lunch the next day, and then chop remaining leftovers into pieces and sauté with eggs for a breakfast hash on day 3. They're also handy when you need to eat on the go. Just wrap them in aluminum foil and pop them into a lunch cooler for a portable, protein-packed, easy-to-eat lunch.

DAIRY-FREE, NUT-FREE, UNDER 30 MINUTES

PREP TIME: 10 minutes
TOTAL COOK TIME: 14 minutes

AIR CRISP: 10 minutes at 370°F

SAUTÉ: 4 minutes

ACCESSORIES: Cook & Crisp™ basket

STORAGE: Store in airtight containers in the refrigerator for up to 4 days or in the freezer for up to 2 months. This dish is best enjoyed during the first few days of your meal planning week. To reheat in the Foodi™, place each portion in the Cook & Crisp™ basket and air crisp at 350°F in 2-minute increments.

- 1 tablespoon extra-virgin olive oil
- 12 ounces skinless salmon fillets
- ½ red bell pepper, diced
- 1 cup panko bread crumbs
- 1 large egg, lightly beaten
- 3 tablespoons mayonnaise
- 2 tablespoons chopped fresh parsley
- ½ teaspoon chopped fresh dill or ¼ teaspoon dried dill
- 1½ teaspoons Old Bay Seasoning or paprika
- ½ teaspoon kosher salt
- ¼ teaspoon freshly ground black pepper
- Nonstick cooking spray

1. Select SEAR/SAUTÉ on your Ninja® Foodi™ and set the temperature to HI. Select START/STOP to begin. Let preheat for 5 minutes

2. Pour the olive oil into the pot. Once the oil is hot, add the salmon and cook for 2 minutes on each side, just until the fish is evenly browned and cooked through. Remove the salmon from the pot and set it aside on a plate to cool slightly. Select START/STOP.

3. In a large bowl, mix together the bell pepper, bread crumbs, egg, mayonnaise, parsley, dill, Old Bay seasoning, salt, and black pepper.

4. When the salmon is cool enough to handle, shred it with two forks. Place the shredded salmon in the bowl with the bread crumb mixture; mix well. Using your hands, form the mixture into 6 round patties of equal size, each one about ½ inch thick.

5. Spray the Cook & Crisp™ basket with cooking spray, then lower the basket into the Foodi™ pot. Place the patties in the basket in one layer. If the patties do not fit in a single layer, work in two batches, placing remaining patties in the refrigerator until you are ready to cook them. Lightly spray the top of each patty with cooking spray.

6. Close the crisping lid. Set the temperature to 370°F, and set the time to 10 minutes. Select START/STOP to begin.

7. After 5 minutes, open the lid and flip the patties over. Close lid to continue crisping for the remaining 5 minutes.

8. When cooking is done, carefully lift the basket out of the pot and plate the salmon patties.

Per serving (2 patties): *Calories: 219; Total fat: 15g; Saturated fat: 3g; Cholesterol: 62mg; Sodium: 261mg; Carbohydrates: 7g; Fiber: 1g; Protein: 14g*

Lemon-Herb Salmon with Asparagus and Rice

Frozen salmon fillets are a smart protein to keep on hand in the freezer. And thanks to the Foodi™, you can cook them straight from the freezer—no need to thaw them first. This appliance has saved me so many times when I've forgotten to defrost meat or when we need to whip up a meal at the last minute. The lemon-herb sauce in this recipe adds a lovely light and bright flavor to the salmon and asparagus.

DAIRY-FREE, GLUTEN-FREE, NUT-FREE, UNDER 30 MINUTES

PREP TIME: 10 minutes
TOTAL COOK TIME: 17 minutes

APPROX. PRESSURE BUILD: 10 minutes
PRESSURE COOK: 2 minutes
PRESSURE RELEASE: natural for 5 minutes, then quick

BROIL: 5 minutes

ACCESSORIES: Deluxe Reversible Rack

- 2 cups water
- 2 cups uncooked jasmine rice, rinsed and drained
- ½ cup extra-virgin olive oil
- 2 garlic cloves, minced
- 2 tablespoons freshly squeezed lemon juice
- ½ tablespoon chopped fresh dill or ¼ teaspoon dried dill
- ½ teaspoon kosher salt
- ¼ teaspoon freshly ground black pepper
- 6 frozen salmon fillets (about 3 pounds total)
- 1 asparagus bunch, trimmed and halved crosswise

1. Pour the water into the pot of your Ninja® Foodi™, add the rice, and stir to combine.

2. In a medium bowl, whisk together the olive oil, garlic, lemon juice, dill, salt, and pepper. Reserve half of the mixture in a separate bowl for later.

3. Brush the salmon on both sides with half of the seasoned olive oil mixture. Place the Deluxe Reversible Rack in the lower steam position without the Deluxe Layer installed and lower it into the pot. Place 3 pieces of salmon on the rack. Next, install the Deluxe Layer on the rack and place the remaining salmon on it.

4. Assemble the pressure lid, making sure the pressure release valve is in the SEAL position. Select PRESSURE and set it to HI. Set the time to 2 minutes. Select START/STOP to begin.

5. While the salmon and rice are cooking, brush the asparagus with the reserved olive oil mixture.

6. When the cooking is complete, quick release the pressure by turning the pressure release valve to the VENT position. Carefully remove the lid when the unit has finished releasing pressure.

7. Carefully lift the rack with the salmon out of the pot. Place the asparagus spears between the salmon on the racks. Carefully return the racks to the pot.

8. Close the crisping lid. Select BROIL and set the time to 7 minutes. Select START/STOP to begin. After 5 minutes, check the salmon for doneness. Cook for the remaining 2 minutes if needed.

9. When the cooking is complete, remove the salmon from the rack and serve with the asparagus and rice.

STORAGE: Refrigerate in airtight containers for up to 3 or 4 days. This salmon dish is best enjoyed earlier in your meal planning week. My favorite way to enjoy leftovers from this dish is to toss salmon and asparagus into a breakfast hash or a quiche.

Per serving: Calories: 645; Total fat: 24g; Saturated fat: 4g; Cholesterol: 125mg; Sodium: 198mg; Carbohydrates: 53g; Fiber: 2g; Protein: 50g

Teriyaki Beef Burgers, *page 176*

6

BEEF AND PORK MAINS

Coffee Short Ribs

SERVES 6

Fall-off-the-bone short ribs in under an hour? Thanks to the Foodi™, it's possible. This is a great dish to make first on meal prep day, since it has a longer cook time than most other recipes in this cookbook. While it's cooking, you can then prep other main courses or sides. Enjoy leftovers served over mac and cheese, mashed potatoes, roasted vegetables, pasta, or on buns as short rib sliders.

DAIRY-FREE, GLUTEN-FREE, NUT-FREE

PREP TIME: 5 minutes
TOTAL COOK TIME: 55 minutes

APPROX. PRESSURE BUILD: 10 minutes
PRESSURE COOK: 35 minutes
PRESSURE RELEASE: natural for 10 minutes, then quick

STORAGE: Store the ribs and sauce in airtight containers in the refrigerator for up to 4 days or in the freezer for up to 3 months.

3 pounds bone-in short ribs

½ teaspoon kosher salt

¼ teaspoon freshly ground black pepper

2 tablespoons extra-virgin olive oil

½ small yellow onion, diced

3 garlic cloves, minced

2 teaspoons chili powder

1 teaspoon dried oregano

½ teaspoon dried thyme

1 cup strong brewed coffee

1 cup dry red wine

1 tablespoon cornstarch (optional)

1 teaspoon water (optional)

1. Select SEAR/SAUTÉ on your Ninja® Foodi™ and set the temperature to HI. Select START/STOP to begin. Let preheat for 5 minutes.

2. Pat the short ribs dry with paper towels. Season with the salt and pepper.

3. Pour the olive oil into the pot. Once the oil is hot, add the short ribs and sear them for 2 to 3 minutes on each side. Set aside on a plate.

4. Add the onion, garlic, chili powder, oregano, and thyme to the Foodi™ pot. Sauté for 1 minute, just until the onion and garlic are soft and fragrant. Scrape up any browned bits from the bottom of the pan as you sauté the onion and garlic.

5. Pour in the coffee and red wine. Return the short ribs to the pot. Select START/STOP.

6. Assemble the pressure lid, making sure the pressure release valve is in the SEAL position. Select PRESSURE and set it to HI. Set the time to 35 minutes. Select START/STOP to begin.

7. When the cooking is complete, allow the pressure to release naturally for 10 minutes. After 10 minutes, quick release the remaining pressure by moving the pressure release valve to the VENT position. Carefully remove the lid when the unit has finished releasing pressure.

8. Optional step: If you would like the sauce to be thicker, transfer the cooked ribs to a plate. Select SEAR/SAUTÉ and set the temperature to HI. Select START/STOP to begin. In a small bowl, whisk together the cornstarch and water until the cornstarch dissolves. Pour the cornstarch mixture into the sauce in the Foodi™ pot; stir until combined. Allow the sauce to thicken, stirring frequently, for 3 to 4 minutes. Return the ribs to the pot and stir gently to coat them with the thickened sauce.

Per serving: *Calories: 362; Total fat: 22g; Saturated fat: 8g; Cholesterol: 87mg; Sodium: 223mg; Carbohydrates: 3g; Fiber: 1g; Protein: 29g*

Pasta with Bacon and Peas

SERVES 6

This is one of my son's favorite Foodi™ meals. It's a simple pasta dish that imparts so much flavor. The crunchy bacon infuses a smoky, salty taste throughout the pasta, and the peas add a touch of brightness and sweetness to the dish. We often make this dairy-free by substituting coconut milk for heavy cream and our favorite dairy-free Parmesan cheese alternative. If you adhere to a gluten-free diet, we've also used gluten-free spaghetti in this recipe with great success.

NUT-FREE, UNDER 30 MINUTES

PREP TIME: 5 minutes
TOTAL COOK TIME: 24 minutes

APPROX. PRESSURE BUILD: 10 minutes
PRESSURE COOK: 3 minutes
PRESSURE RELEASE: natural for 5 minutes, then quick

SAUTÉ: 6 minutes

STORAGE: Store in airtight containers in the refrigerator for up to 4 days or in the freezer for up to 1 month. If freezing, do so before adding the heavy cream and Parmesan cheese. When you are ready to eat, thaw and heat on Sauté function, and continue with step 8.

6 slices bacon, cut into small pieces

1 small yellow onion, diced

1 garlic clove, minced

4½ cups chicken broth, divided

12 ounces spaghetti

½ cup heavy (whipping) cream or half-and-half

¼ cup grated Parmesan cheese

1 cup frozen peas

1 tablespoon chopped fresh basil (optional)

1. Select SEAR/SAUTÉ on your Ninja® Foodi™ and set the temperature to HI. Select START/STOP to begin. Let preheat for 5 minutes.

2. Place the bacon in the pot and sauté for about 3 to 4 minutes, stirring constantly, until cooked to your desired crispness. Transfer the bacon to a paper towel–lined plate. Set aside. Pour out some of the fat, leaving about 1 tablespoon of bacon grease in the pot.

3. Add the onion and garlic to the Foodi™ pot and sauté for 1 to 2 minutes, just until soft and fragrant. Select START/STOP.

4. Pour a bit of the chicken broth into the pot, then use a wooden spoon to scrape up any browned bits from the bottom of the pot.

5. Place the spaghetti in the pot in overlapping layers. You may need to break the pasta in half to make it fit inside the pot. Pour the remaining chicken broth over the pasta, then gently press the pasta down to submerge it in the liquid.

6. Assemble the pressure lid, making sure the pressure release valve is in the SEAL position. Select PRESSURE and set it to HI. Set the time to 3 minutes. Select START/STOP to begin.

7. When the cooking is complete, allow the pressure to release naturally for 5 minutes. After 5 minutes, quick release the remaining pressure by moving the pressure release valve to the VENT position. Carefully remove the lid when the unit has finished releasing pressure.

8. Stir in the heavy cream, Parmesan cheese, and peas. The residual heat will thaw and warm up the peas in about 1 minute. Garnish with the basil (if using).

Per serving: *Calories: 377; Total fat: 13g; Saturated fat: 7g; Cholesterol: 43mg; Sodium: 858mg; Carbohydrates: 49g; Fiber: 3g; Protein: 14g*

Teriyaki Beef Burgers

If you've never made burgers in the Foodi™ before, you will love how easy it is—not just the cooking part, but the cleanup, too. Cleaning a grill is one of my least favorite cooking chores after grilling burgers, but the Foodi™ is so easy to clean that I no longer hesitate when the family suggests burgers for dinner. Flavorful teriyaki beef burgers are a delicious Asian-inspired, tropical twist on this classic family favorite.

DAIRY-FREE, NUT-FREE, UNDER 30 MINUTES

PREP TIME: 10 minutes
TOTAL COOK TIME: 8 minutes

AIR CRISP: 5 minutes at 400°F

SAUTÉ: 3 minutes

ACCESSORIES: Deluxe Reversible Rack

VARIATION TIP:
To enhance the Asian-inspired flavors, try serving the burgers with rice vinegar slaw and hoisin or teriyaki sauce instead of ketchup and mustard. Chop up leftover burgers for a ramen noodle lunch.

- 2 pounds 80% lean ground beef
- 1 tablespoon minced garlic (about 2 garlic cloves)
- 1 tablespoon minced fresh ginger
- 2 teaspoons sesame oil
- ¼ cup soy sauce or coconut aminos
- 2 teaspoons finely sliced scallions
- 1 teaspoon kosher salt
- ½ teaspoon freshly ground black pepper
- 6 slices pineapple
- 6 hamburger buns

1. Select SEAR/SAUTÉ on your Ninja® Foodi™ and set the temperature to HI. Select START/STOP to begin. Let preheat for 5 minutes.

2. Meanwhile, in a large bowl, mix together the ground beef, garlic, ginger, sesame oil, soy sauce, scallions, salt, and pepper. Form 6 burger patties of similar size, each one about 1 inch thick.

3. Place the patties in the Foodi™ pot in a single layer. If they do not all fit in one layer, you may need to work in batches. Sear the patties for 2 to 3 minutes per side, until browned. Select START/STOP.

4. Place the Deluxe Reversible Rack in the lower steam position without the Deluxe Layer installed and lower the rack into the Foodi™ pot. Place 3 burgers on the rack. Next, install the Deluxe Layer on the rack and place the remaining burgers on it.

5. Close the crisping lid. Select AIR CRISP, set the temperature to 400ºF, and set the time to 5 minutes. Select START/STOP to begin.

6. When the cooking is complete, open the lid and remove the burgers. The burgers are fully cooked when their internal temperature reads 130ºF to 135ºF for medium-rare, 150ºF to 155ºF for medium-well, or 160ºF to 165ºF for well done on a food thermometer.

7. Place a slice of pineapple on top of each burger, and place the topped patties between hamburger buns to serve.

Per serving: *Calories: 434; Total fat: 18g; Saturated fat: 7g; Cholesterol: 98mg; Sodium: 887mg; Carbohydrates: 30g; Fiber: 1g; Protein: 36g*

STORAGE: Wrap each burger individually in plastic wrap or aluminum foil, then transfer to airtight containers and refrigerate for up to 4 days or freeze for up to 1 month.

Classic Beef Tacos

SERVES 6

It's never been faster to get Taco Tuesday meals onto the table, thanks to the Foodi™. At home, I make this with ground beef or ground turkey—any ground meat you have in your freezer will work. Once you have the taco meat cooked, you can then portion it out in so many ways for your meal prep week: After enjoying it in tacos, make huevos rancheros for breakfast the next morning, make a taco salad for lunch on day 3, and use it for taco pizza toppings for a dinner later in the week. There are many creative and fun possibilities.

DAIRY-FREE, NUT-FREE

PREP TIME: 5 minutes
TOTAL COOK TIME: 40 minutes

APPROX. PRESSURE BUILD: 10 minutes
PRESSURE COOK: 15 minutes
PRESSURE RELEASE: natural for 10 minutes, then quick

SAUTÉ: 5 minutes

STORAGE: Store the meat on its own in airtight containers in the refrigerator for up to 4 days or in the freezer for up to 3 months.

1 cup water, divided
1 pound ground beef
¼ cup taco seasoning
6 taco shells or flour tortillas

Shredded lettuce, shredded cheddar cheese, salsa, sour cream, chopped fresh cilantro (optional)

1. Pour ½ cup of water into the inner pot of your Ninja® Foodi™. Add the ground beef to the pot, then stir in the taco seasoning.

2. Assemble the pressure lid, making sure the pressure release valve is in the SEAL position. Select PRESSURE and set it to HI. Set the time to 15 minutes. Select START/STOP to begin.

3. When the cooking is complete, allow the pressure to release naturally for 10 minutes. After 10 minutes, quick release the remaining pressure by moving the pressure release valve to the VENT position. Carefully remove the lid when the unit has finished releasing pressure.

4. Select SEAR/SAUTÉ and set the temperature to HI. Select START/STOP to begin. Pour the remaining ½ cup of water into the pot and stir, breaking up the meat with a wooden spoon. Cook until almost all the liquid has evaporated, up to 5 minutes.

5. Serve with taco shells or flour tortillas. Add your choice of toppings, including shredded lettuce, shredded cheese, salsa, sour cream, or cilantro (if using).

Per serving: *Calories: 348; Total fat: 18g; Saturated fat: 6g; Cholesterol: 54mg; Sodium: 794mg; Carbohydrates: 27g; Fiber: 2g; Protein: 17g*

Stuffed Pork Tenderloin

We used to only make stuffed pork tenderloin for dinner parties or holiday feasts. Now, with the Foodi™, we can enjoy this delicious, elegant dinner even on the busiest weeknight. Pressure cooking allows the pork to cook quickly from the inside out, so it stays tender and juicy. And because you can portion it out easily, stuffed pork tenderloin is a great meal prep recipe to have in your rotation.

DAIRY-FREE, GLUTEN-FREE, NUT-FREE

PREP TIME: 10 minutes
TOTAL COOK TIME: 29 minutes

APPROX. PRESSURE BUILD: 10 minutes
PRESSURE COOK: 5 minutes
PRESSURE RELEASE: natural for 10 minutes, then quick

SAUTÉ: 4 minutes

ACCESSORIES: Deluxe Reversible Rack

VARIATION TIP: You can get creative with the filling for this recipe. If you prefer a thinner filling, try a pesto sauce with chopped mushrooms.

4 slices bacon, chopped
½ small onion, diced
2 garlic cloves, minced
¼ cup chopped fresh parsley
½ teaspoons sea salt
½ teaspoon freshly ground black pepper
1 (1- to 1¼-pound) pork tenderloin
Nonstick cooking spray
½ cup apple cider

1. Select SEAR/SAUTÉ on your Ninja® Foodi™ and set the temperature to HI. Select START/STOP to begin. Let preheat for 5 minutes.

2. Place the bacon in the pot and cook for 2 minutes or until the fat has just started to render. Stir in the onion, garlic, parsley, salt, and pepper and sauté for 2 more minutes, just until the onion and garlic are soft and fragrant. Select START/STOP, then transfer the ingredients to a medium bowl.

3. Using a sharp knife, slice the pork horizontally along the long side, cutting almost to the center of the meat, and then open the meat like a book. If your tenderloin is thicker than ½ inch at this point, cover it with plastic wrap and pound it with a meat mallet, rolling pin, or potato masher until the meat is about ½-inch thick.

4. Spoon the bacon-herb mixture evenly over the center of the pork tenderloin, leaving a ½-inch margin around the edges. Working from one longest side to the other, roll the pork to the end; secure the seams with toothpicks to hold the roll in place while cooking.

5. Spray the Deluxe Reversible Rack with cooking spray. Pour the apple cider into the pot. Place the Deluxe Reversible Rack in the lower steam position without the Deluxe Layer installed and lower the rack into the Foodi™ pot. Place the tenderloin on the rack. You may need to curve the ends of the tenderloin into a "c" shape so it fits on the rack.

6. Assemble the pressure lid, making sure the pressure release valve is in the SEAL position. Select PRESSURE and set it to HI. Set the time to 5 minutes. Select START/STOP to begin.

7. When the cooking is complete, allow the pressure to release naturally for 10 minutes. After 10 minutes, quick release the remaining pressure by moving the pressure release valve to the VENT position. Carefully remove the lid when the unit has finished releasing pressure.

8. Cooking is complete when the internal temperature of the meat reads at least 145ºF on a food thermometer.

Per serving: Calories: 129; Total fat: 5g; Saturated fat: 2g; Cholesterol: 55mg; Sodium: 257mg; Carbohydrates: 1g; Fiber: 0g; Protein: 18g

STORAGE: Store in airtight containers in the refrigerator for up to 4 days or in the freezer for up to 1 month.

Cheeseburger Pasta

Talk about a family favorite comfort food. This recipe is a nod to Hamburger Helper, a popular boxed pasta product that was introduced in the United States in the early 1970s in response to a meat shortage. This modern version is packed with flavors from the fresh aromatics and herbs, but it still has that nostalgic, magic combo of pasta with ground meat, cheese, and cream.

NUT-FREE

PREP TIME: 10 minutes
TOTAL COOK TIME:
21 minutes

APPROX. PRESSURE
BUILD: 10 minutes
PRESSURE COOK:
5 minutes
PRESSURE RELEASE:
quick

SAUTÉ: 6 minutes

VARIATION TIP: To wake up leftovers in your meal plan week, try heating this dish up with some coconut milk or additional beef broth to create Cheeseburger Pasta Soup. You can also place it in a Foodi™ all-purpose pan, top it with extra cheese and herbs, and bake it in the Foodi™ to create a yummy pasta bake.

---

1 tablespoon extra-virgin olive oil

1 pound lean ground beef

½ cup diced yellow or white onion

2 garlic cloves, minced

1 teaspoon paprika

½ teaspoon dried oregano

1 teaspoon Dijon mustard

12 ounces elbow macaroni

1 (14.5-ounce) can tomato sauce

3 cups beef broth

2 cups shredded cheddar cheese

½ cup heavy (whipping) cream or half-and-half

1 tablespoon chopped fresh parsley (optional)

1. Select SEAR/SAUTÉ on your Ninja® Foodi™ and set the temperature to HI. Select START/STOP to begin. Let preheat for 5 minutes.

2. Pour the olive oil into the pot. Once the oil is hot, add the beef and sauté until it is evenly browned, 4 to 5 minutes. Stir in the onion, garlic, paprika, oregano, and mustard and sauté for 1 more minute. Select START/STOP.

3. Layer the macaroni on top of the beef and vegetables. Pour in the tomato sauce, then the beef broth. Gently push the pasta down so most of the noodles are submerged in the liquid.

4. Assemble the pressure lid, making sure the pressure release valve is in the SEAL position. Select PRESSURE and set it to HI. Set the time to 5 minutes. Select START/STOP to begin.

5. When the cooking is complete, quick release the pressure by turning the pressure release valve to the VENT position. Carefully remove the lid when the unit has finished releasing pressure.

6. Stir in the cheese and heavy cream, and garnish with the chopped parsley (if using).

Per serving: Calories: 514; Total fat: 25g; Saturated fat: 12g; Cholesterol: 87mg; Sodium: 769mg; Carbohydrates: 46g; Fiber: 4g; Protein: 27g

STORAGE: Store in airtight containers in the refrigerator for up to 4 days or in the freezer for up to 1 month.

Italian Sausage Pasta

Every home cook needs a hearty pasta recipe in their back pocket, and this one is a family favorite. The Foodi™ creates a rich homemade sauce that tastes as if it has been simmering all day on the stove—but really only takes 8 minutes of pressure cooking along with the meat and pasta.

DAIRY-FREE, NUT-FREE

PREP TIME: 5 minutes
TOTAL COOK TIME: 34 minutes

APPROX. PRESSURE BUILD: 10 minutes
PRESSURE COOK: 8 minutes
PRESSURE RELEASE: natural for 10 minutes, then quick

SAUTÉ: 6 minutes

STORAGE: Store in airtight containers in the refrigerator for up to 4 days or in the freezer for up to 3 months.

- 2 tablespoons extra-virgin olive oil
- 2 garlic cloves, minced
- 1 small onion, diced
- 1 pound ground mild Italian sausage
- ½ teaspoon kosher salt
- ¼ teaspoon freshly ground black pepper
- 1 cup water
- 1 (14.5-ounce) can beef broth
- 1 (14.5-ounce) can diced tomatoes
- 1 (6-ounce) can tomato paste
- 1 tablespoon chopped fresh basil
- 1 teaspoon dried thyme
- 12 ounces rigatoni, ziti, or penne

1. Select SEAR/SAUTÉ on your Ninja® Foodi™ and set the temperature to HI. Select START/STOP to begin.

2. Pour the oil into the pot. Once the oil is hot, add the garlic and onion and sauté for 1 minute, just until fragrant and soft. Add the Italian sausage to the pot and season with the salt and pepper. Sauté for 4 to 5 minutes, stirring constantly to break up the meat and ensure even browning. Once the meat has browned, select START/STOP.

3. Pour the water and beef broth into the pot, followed by the diced tomatoes, tomato paste, basil, and thyme. Stir to combine, then place the pasta evenly on top of the ingredients in the pot. Gently press down on the pasta until most of the noodles are submerged in the liquid.

4. Assemble the pressure lid, making sure the pressure release valve is in the SEAL position. Select PRESSURE and set it to HI. Set the time to 8 minutes. Select START/STOP to begin.

5. When the cooking is complete, allow the pressure to release naturally for 10 minutes. After 10 minutes, quick release the remaining pressure by moving the pressure release valve to the VENT position. Carefully remove the lid when the unit has finished releasing pressure.

6. Stir well before serving.

Per serving: *Calories: 557; Total fat: 29g; Saturated fat: 9g; Cholesterol: 59mg; Sodium: 928mg; Carbohydrates: 52g; Fiber: 5g; Protein: 21g*

Pork Chops and Rice

Even though pork chops may be viewed as the main event in this recipe, I think you'll really love how flavorful the rice is. Because the rice cooks at the same time as the seasoned pork chops, those fragrant seasonings make their way into every tender grain. To save time, I use boneless pork chops and onion and garlic powders. If you have a few more minutes, try this recipe with bone-in pork chops, minced fresh garlic, and diced onion.

DAIRY-FREE, GLUTEN-FREE, NUT-FREE

PREP TIME: 5 minutes
TOTAL COOK TIME: 29 minutes

APPROX. PRESSURE BUILD: 10 minutes
PRESSURE COOK: 8 minutes
PRESSURE RELEASE: natural for 5 minutes, then quick

SAUTÉ: 4 minutes

ACCESSORIES: Deluxe Reversible Rack

STORAGE: Store in airtight containers in the refrigerator for up to 4 days or in the freezer for up to 2 months.

6 boneless pork chops (1½ to 2 pounds total)
1 teaspoon paprika
1 teaspoon garlic powder
1 teaspoon onion powder
½ teaspoon kosher salt
¼ teaspoon freshly ground black pepper
2 tablespoons extra-virgin olive oil
2 cups chicken broth or water
2 cups white rice

1. Select SEAR/SAUTÉ on your Ninja® Foodi™ and set the temperature to HI. Select START/STOP to begin. Let preheat for 5 minutes.

2. Meanwhile, season the pork chops on both sides with the paprika, garlic powder, onion powder, salt, and pepper.

3. Pour the olive oil into the pot. Once the oil is hot, add the pork chops and cook for about 2 minutes per side, just until lightly browned. Transfer the chops to a plate and set aside. You may need to work in batches, depending on how many pork chops fit in your Foodi™ pot at one time.

4. Pour the broth into the pot. Using a wooden spoon, scrape up any browned bits from the bottom of the pot. Pour the rice into the pot, and stir to submerge the rice in the liquid.

5. Place the Deluxe Reversible Rack in the lower steam position without the Deluxe Layer installed and lower it into the Foodi™ pot over the rice and liquid. Place 3 pork chops on the rack. Next, install the Deluxe Layer on the rack and place the remaining pork chops on it.

6. Assemble the pressure lid, making sure the pressure release valve is in the SEAL position. Select PRESSURE and set it to HI. Set the time to 8 minutes. Select START/STOP to begin.

7. When the cooking is complete, allow the pressure to naturally release for 7 minutes. After 7 minutes, quick release the remaining pressure by moving the pressure release valve to the VENT position. Carefully remove the lid when the unit has finished releasing pressure.

8. Lift the rack out of the Foodi™ and plate the pork chops. Use a fork to fluff up the rice.

Per serving: Calories: 458; Total fat: 13g; Saturated fat: 4g; Cholesterol: 76mg; Sodium: 153mg; Carbohydrates: 54g; Fiber: 2g; Protein: 29g

Rosemary-Garlic Sausage and Potatoes

Recipes like this are made for busy weeknights and meal planning. All of the ingredients cook together at the same time, getting nice and crispy in the Foodi™. Once you've made this, try experimenting with different bratwurst flavors and adding different spices to the potatoes. I also like to serve this with a variety of mustards, sauerkraut, and side of coleslaw.

DAIRY-FREE, GLUTEN-FREE, NUT-FREE, UNDER 30 MINUTES

PREP TIME: 10 minutes
TOTAL COOK TIME: 12 minutes

AIR CRISP: 12 minutes at 400°F

ACCESSORIES: Cook & Crisp™ basket

VARIATION TIP: Leftovers make an excellent breakfast hash. You can also finely chop the sausage, potatoes, and onion and use them as pizza toppings or a calzone filling.

6 bratwurst links, cut into 1-inch-thick slices

3 baking potatoes, cut into small cubes

½ cup diced yellow onion

2 tablespoons extra-virgin olive oil

1 garlic clove, minced

2 teaspoons chopped fresh rosemary

½ teaspoon kosher salt

¼ teaspoon freshly ground black pepper

1. Place the Cook & Crisp™ basket in the inner pot of your Ninja® Foodi™, then close the crisping lid.

2. Select AIR CRISP, set the temperature to 400°F, and set the time to 5 minutes. Select START/STOP to begin preheating.

3. Meanwhile, in a large bowl, toss together the bratwurst, potatoes, onion, olive oil, garlic, and rosemary. Season with the salt and pepper.

4. Once the Foodi™ has finished preheating, open the lid and place the ingredients in the basket.

5. Close the crisping lid. Select AIR CRISP, set the temperature to 400°F, and set the time to 12 minutes. Select START/STOP to begin.

6. After 6 minutes, open the lid and use tongs or a wooden spoon to gently toss the ingredients. Close the lid to resume cooking. Cooking is complete when the internal temperature of the bratwurst reads at least 160°F on a food thermometer and the potatoes are cooked to your preferred crispiness.

Per serving: *Calories: 413; Total fat: 29g; Saturated fat: 9g; Cholesterol: 63mg; Sodium: 829;mg; Carbohydrates: 22g; Fiber: 2g; Protein: 14g*

STORAGE: Store in airtight containers in the refrigerator for up to 4 days or in the freezer for up to 1 month.

Stromboli

This thick, hearty Italian American creation was invented in Philadelphia It is similar to a calzone, but instead of being folded, it's rolled like a burrito and then sliced. You can use any of your favorite deli meats in this dish, and feel free to experiment with other favorite cheeses, too. This is an awesome meal prep recipe that comes together quickly and easily.

NUT-FREE, UNDER 30 MINUTES

PREP TIME: 10 minutes
TOTAL COOK TIME: 10 minutes

AIR CRISP: 10 minutes at 375°F

ACCESSORIES: Deluxe Reversible Rack

STORAGE: Wrap in aluminum foil and store in the refrigerator for up to 4 days or in the freezer for up to 2 months.

- 1 (13.8-ounce) container refrigerated pizza dough
- ½ cup pizza sauce
- 24 slices pepperoni
- 1 cup plus 2 tablespoons shredded Italian-blend or mozzarella cheese, divided
- ½ teaspoon dried oregano
- ½ teaspoon dried basil
- 24 slices salami
- 1 large egg, lightly beaten
- 1 tablespoon water
- 1 tablespoon chopped fresh parsley
- Nonstick cooking spray

1. Roll the dough into a 10-by-13-inch rectangle, with the long side facing you.

2. Spread the pizza sauce across the dough, leaving a 1-inch margin around the edges. Place the pepperoni evenly on top of the sauce. Sprinkle 1 cup of cheese evenly over the pepperoni. Sprinkle oregano and basil evenly over the cheese, then top with the salami slices.

3. Starting at the long side of the rectangle, roll the dough into a long cylinder. As you roll, carefully push in any meat or cheese pieces that try to escape. Using a sharp knife, cut the roll in half lengthwise, then tuck in all the edges to seal.

CONTINUED ▶

4. In a small bowl, whisk together the egg and water. Brush the egg wash over all sides of the dough rolls. This helps seal the edges and gives the stromboli a nice golden color when crisped. Cut 2 to 3 small (½-inch-deep) slits across the top of each roll. Sprinkle the remaining 2 tablespoons of cheese and the parsley over the tops.

5. Spray the Deluxe Reversible Rack with cooking spray. Place the reversible rack in the lower steam position without the Deluxe Layer installed and lower the rack into the Foodi™ pot. Place the filled rolls on the rack.

6. Close the crisping lid. Select AIR CRISP, set the temperature to 375°F, and set the time to 10 minutes. Select START/STOP to begin.

7. After 5 minutes, check on the stromboli. If the cheese on top is starting to burn, carefully lift out the rack, flip both stromboli, and return the rack to the pot. Close the lid and resume cooking for the remaining 5 minutes.

8. When the cooking is complete, open the lid and carefully lift out the rack. Let the stromboli cool for 2 to 5 minutes, then slice them into 6 servings.

Per serving: Calories: 362; Total fat: 17g; Saturated fat: 7g; Cholesterol: 75mg; Sodium: 942mg; Carbohydrates: 35g; Fiber: 2g; Protein: 18g

Kalbi (Korean-Style Beef Short Ribs)

SERVES 6

With the Foodi™, you can make restaurant-quality Korean short ribs in less time. You can substitute sweet marsala wine, cooking sherry, or dry white wine for the mirin.

DAIRY-FREE, NUT-FREE, ONE AND DONE

PREP TIME: 10 minutes
TOTAL COOK TIME: 45 minutes

APPROX. PRESSURE BUILD: 10 minutes
PRESSURE COOK: 25 minutes
PRESSURE RELEASE: natural for 10 minutes, then quick

VARIATION TIP: Grating an Asian pear into the sauce adds flavor and helps tenderize the meat. If you can't find an Asian pear, you can substitute a common Bartlett, Anjou, or Bosc pear instead.

STORAGE: Store in airtight containers in the refrigerator for up to 4 days or in the freezer for up to 2 months.

½ cup soy sauce
¼ cup water
¼ tablespoon mirin
1 (1-inch) piece fresh ginger, grated
½ small yellow onion, diced
2 garlic cloves, minced
½ Asian pear, peeled and grated
1 tablespoon toasted sesame oil
4 tablespoons brown sugar
¼ teaspoon freshly ground black pepper
2 pounds bone-in beef short ribs
2 scallions, sliced thinly (optional)

1. Pour the soy sauce, water, and mirin into the pot. Stir in the ginger, onion, garlic, Asian pear, sesame oil, brown sugar, and black pepper. Add the ribs; toss to coat.

2. Assemble the pressure lid, making sure the pressure release valve is in the SEAL position. Select PRESSURE and set it to HI. Set the time to 25 minutes. Select START/STOP to begin.

3. When the cooking is complete, allow the pressure to release naturally for 10 minutes. After 10 minutes, quick release the remaining pressure by moving the pressure release valve to the VENT position. Carefully remove the lid when the unit has finished releasing pressure.

4. Using tongs, transfer the ribs to a plate; be careful, since they should be tender and may literally fall off the bone. Spoon the sauce from the pot over the ribs and toss to coat. When ready to serve, garnish with the scallions (if using).

Per serving: Calories: 352; Total fat: 19g; Saturated fat: 7g; Cholesterol: 86mg; Sodium: 869mg; Carbohydrates: 9g; Fiber: 1g; Protein: 31g

Butternut Squash Mac and Cheese, *page 205*

7

VEGETARIAN MAINS AND SIDES

Pasta Primavera

If you've got some veggies in the refrigerator that you need to use up or you're simply looking for more ways to incorporate vegetables into your day, it's Pasta Primavera to the rescue. This is such a versatile dish: You can use almost any vegetable you happen to have on hand. If you like, sprinkle on some grated Parmesan cheese just before serving for a delicious, cheesy finish.

DAIRY-FREE, NUT-FREE, UNDER 30 MINUTES, VEGAN

PREP TIME: 10 minutes
TOTAL COOK TIME: 19 minutes

APPROX. PRESSURE BUILD: 10 minutes
PRESSURE COOK: 5 minutes
PRESSURE RELEASE: quick

SAUTÉ: 4 minutes

VARIATION TIP: This pasta is also great with zucchini, butternut squash, asparagus, or corn. Whichever vegetables you use, try to chop them so they are similar in size and cook evenly together.

2 tablespoons extra-virgin olive oil

2 garlic cloves, minced

1 cup chopped broccoli

1 red bell pepper, diced

2 cups cherry tomatoes, halved and seeded

½ cup peas

½ teaspoon kosher salt

¼ teaspoon freshly ground black pepper

2 cups vegetable broth or water

12 ounces short pasta, like penne, fusilli, or rotini

1 tablespoon chopped fresh basil

1. Select SEAR/SAUTÉ on your Ninja® Foodi™ and set the temperature to HI. Select START/STOP to begin. Let preheat for 5 minutes.

2. Pour the olive oil into the pot. Once the oil is hot, add the garlic and sauté for 1 minute, just until fragrant and softened. Stir in the broccoli, bell pepper, tomatoes, and peas, and season with the salt and pepper. Sauté for 3 to 4 minutes, just until the broccoli and peppers are slightly softened. Select START/STOP. Transfer the vegetables to a bowl, and cover them with aluminum foil to keep warm.

3. Pour a little of the vegetable broth into the pot, then use a wooden spoon to scrape up any browned bits from the bottom of the pot. Spread the pasta across the bottom of the pot, and pour in the remaining broth. Gently press down on the pasta so it is submerged in the liquid, but do not stir.

4. Assemble the pressure lid, making sure the pressure release valve is in the SEAL position. Select PRESSURE and set it to HI. Set the time to 5 minutes. Select START/STOP to begin.

5. When the cooking is complete, quick release the pressure by turning the pressure release valve to the VENT position. Carefully remove the lid when the unit has finished releasing pressure.

6. Gently stir the vegetables into the pasta. Sprinkle with the basil and toss lightly before serving.

Per serving: Calories: 282; Total fat: 6g; Saturated fat: 0g; Cholesterol: 0mg; Sodium: 109mg; Carbohydrates: 49g; Fiber: 4g; Protein: 9g

STORAGE: Store in airtight containers in the refrigerator for up to 4 days or in the freezer for up to 1 month. To reheat in the Foodi™, select SEAR/SAUTÉ and set the temperature to MD:HI. Select START/STOP to begin. Pour 1 tablespoon of extra-virgin olive oil into the pot. Once the oil is hot, stir in one portion of pasta primavera. Stir frequently as the pasta and vegetables heat up. If the pasta seems dry, stir in 1 tablespoon of water at a time until it reaches your desired consistency. To reheat in the microwave, add a little bit of water and/or olive oil to each serving, then heat in 1-minute increments until hot.

Mushroom Risotto

Achieve creamy, cheesy risotto in less than half the time it typically takes to cook it on the stove top. Instead of standing over a pot, continuously stirring the rice, you simply combine the ingredients in the Foodi™, and the appliance does the hard work for you. My family loves making this for Meatless Mondays.

GLUTEN-FREE, NUT-FREE, VEGETARIAN

PREP TIME: 10 minutes
TOTAL COOK TIME: 25 minutes

APPROX. PRESSURE BUILD: 10 minutes
PRESSURE COOK: 5 minutes
PRESSURE RELEASE: natural for 5 minutes, then quick

SAUTÉ: 10 minutes

VARIATION TIP: Make this dairy-free by substituting your favorite dairy-free cheese alternative for the Parmesan.

STORAGE: Store in airtight containers in the refrigerator for up to 4 days or in the freezer for up to 1 month. Before reheating, add 1 teaspoon of water per serving to help fluff up the rice.

- 2 tablespoons unsalted butter
- 1 shallot, finely chopped
- 3 garlic cloves, minced
- 1 cup sliced cremini mushrooms
- 1 tablespoon fresh thyme leaves
- 2 cups Arborio rice
- ¼ cup dry white wine
- 2 (14.5-ounce) cans vegetable broth or water (about 4 cups)
- 1 teaspoon grated lemon zest
- ¾ cup freshly grated Parmesan cheese
- ½ cup peas (if frozen, no need to thaw)
- ¼ teaspoon kosher salt
- ¼ teaspoon freshly ground black pepper

1. Select SEAR/SAUTÉ on your Ninja® Foodi™ and set the temperature to HI. Select START/STOP to begin. Let preheat for 5 minutes.

2. Place the butter in the pot. Once the butter has completely melted, add the shallot and garlic and sauté for 2 to 3 minutes, just until fragrant and softened. Stir in the mushrooms and thyme and cook for 1 more minute. Add the rice and stir for 2 minutes, just until lightly toasted.

3. Pour in the wine, then use a wooden spoon to scrape up any browned bits from the bottom of the pot. Cook for 3 to 4 minutes, until most of the wine is absorbed. Add the broth and lemon zest and stir for 1 minute. Select START/STOP.

4. Assemble the pressure lid, making sure the pressure release valve is in the SEAL position. Select PRESSURE and set it to HI. Set the time to 5 minutes. Select START/STOP to begin.

5. When the cooking is complete, quick release the pressure by turning the pressure release valve to the VENT position. Carefully remove the lid when the unit has finished releasing pressure.

6. Stir in the Parmesan cheese and peas, and season with the salt and pepper before serving or storing.

Per serving: *Calories: 339; Total fat: 8g; Saturated fat: 4g; Cholesterol: 21mg; Sodium: 284mg; Carbohydrates: 55g; Fiber: 3g; Protein: 9g*

Tabbouleh

This Middle Eastern grain salad is both delicious and nutritious. Bulgur has a slightly nutty flavor and chewy texture, making it great for satisfying salads. However, you can use quinoa or farro instead.

DAIRY-FREE, NUT-FREE, VEGAN

PREP TIME: 10 minutes
TOTAL COOK TIME: 23 minutes

APPROX. PRESSURE BUILD: 10 minutes
PRESSURE COOK: 3 minutes
PRESSURE RELEASE: natural for 10 minutes, then quick

STORAGE: Store in airtight containers in the refrigerator for up to 4 days or in the freezer for up to 1 month.

1 cup bulgur wheat
½ teaspoon ground cumin
2 cups vegetable broth or water
1½ teaspoon kosher salt, divided
1 large cucumber, seeded and diced
3 Roma tomatoes, seeded and diced
½ cup chopped fresh parsley
1 tablespoon chopped fresh mint
⅓ cup extra-virgin olive oil
¼ cup freshly squeezed lemon juice
¼ teaspoon freshly ground black pepper

1. Place the bulger in the pot, then sprinkle the cumin evenly over top. Add in the broth and 1 teaspoon of salt.

2. Assemble the pressure lid, making sure the valve is in the SEAL position. Select PRESSURE, set it to HI, and set the time to 3 minutes. Select START/STOP to begin.

3. When the cooking is complete, allow the pressure to release naturally for 10 minutes. After 10 minutes, quick release the remaining pressure by turning the pressure release valve to the VENT position. Carefully remove the lid when the unit has finished releasing pressure.

4. Transfer the bulgur to a bowl, and cool completely. Add remaining ingredients; toss gently to combine.

Per serving: Calories: 208; Total fat: 12g; Saturated fat: 2g; Cholesterol: 0mg; Sodium: 302mg; Carbohydrates: 23g; Fiber: 4g; Protein: 4g

Mexican-Style Street Corn

This recipe is a nod to Mexican street corn, one of my favorite international street foods. In Mexico, elote *(meaning "corn" in Spanish) is grilled and slathered with butter, mayonnaise, cotija cheese, and chili powder, then served on a stick for easy on-the-go snacking. This is a great side dish to accompany any of the other recipes in this cookbook, or a satisfying, light lunch on its own.*

GLUTEN-FREE, NUT-FREE, UNDER 30 MINUTES, VEGETARIAN

PREP TIME: 10 minutes
TOTAL COOK TIME: 14 minutes

APPROX. PRESSURE BUILD: 10 minutes
PRESSURE COOK: 2 minutes
PRESSURE RELEASE: quick

AIR CRISP: 2 minutes at 400°F

ACCESSORIES: Deluxe Reversible Rack

VARIATION TIP: Though most butter and mayonnaise are gluten-free, always check the label to be sure. If you are not vegetarian, try adding crumbled bacon bits on top of the corn for additional salty crunch.

1 cup water

6 ears corn on the cob, husks removed

3 tablespoons unsalted butter

¼ cup mayonnaise

¼ cup sour cream

1 tablespoon freshly squeezed lime juice

¼ teaspoon paprika or chili powder

½ teaspoon garlic powder

¼ cup cotija cheese

¼ cup chopped fresh cilantro

1. Pour the water into the inner pot of your Ninja® Foodi™. Slather each ear of corn with the butter. Place the Deluxe Reversible Rack in the lower steam position without the Deluxe Layer installed and lower the rack into the Foodi™ pot. Place 3 ears of corn on the rack. Next, install the Deluxe Layer on the rack and place the remaining ears of corn on it.

2. Assemble the pressure lid, making sure the pressure release valve is in the SEAL position. Select PRESSURE and set it to HI. Set the time to 2 minutes. Select START/STOP to begin.

3. Meanwhile, in a medium bowl, mix together the mayonnaise, sour cream, lime juice, paprika, and garlic powder. Set aside.

4. When the cooking is complete, quick release the pressure by turning the pressure release valve to the VENT position. Carefully remove the lid when the unit has finished releasing pressure.

CONTINUED ▶

Mexican-Style Street Corn continued

PREP TIP: To make ahead, complete steps 1 through 8. Then, wrap individual ears of corn in aluminum foil and place the prepared mayonnaise mixture in a separate airtight container. Refrigerate for up to 4 days. To reheat in the Foodi™, place the corn on the Deluxe Reversible Rack and close the crisping lid. Select AIR CRISP, set the temperature to 375°F, and set the time to 4 minutes. Select START/STOP to begin. When cooking is complete, continue with step 9.

5. Lift the rack out of the Foodi™ and set aside. Pour out any remaining water from the pot, then return the pot to the Foodi™.

6. Return the reversible rack with the corn to the Foodi™ pot. Close the crisping lid. Select AIR CRISP, set the temperature to 400°F, and set the time to 2 minutes. Select START/STOP to begin.

7. When the cooking is done, remove the rack from the Foodi™ and transfer the corn to individual plates.

8. Slather the corn with the mayonnaise–sour cream mixture, then sprinkle the cotija cheese and cilantro evenly over each ear of corn.

Per serving: Calories: 271; Total fat: 17g; Saturated fat: 7g; Cholesterol: 28mg; Sodium: 112mg; Carbohydrates: 30g; Fiber: 4g; Protein: 5g

Corn and Tomato Couscous

This light vegan dish sings of summer, but the pearl couscous (also known as Israeli couscous) makes it hearty enough to enjoy during colder months, too. It's perfectly packable for picnics and barbecues, so it is excellent for meal planning. Though this recipe is great on its own, you can also serve it on top of a bed of mixed greens or add your favorite protein. I love adding shrimp to this dish, although it's decidedly not vegan.

DAIRY-FREE, NUT-FREE, UNDER 30 MINUTES, VEGAN

PREP TIME: 5 minutes
TOTAL COOK TIME: 22 minutes

APPROX. PRESSURE BUILD: 10 minutes
PRESSURE COOK: 1 minute
PRESSURE RELEASE: natural for 10 minutes, then quick

SAUTÉ: 1 minute

VARIATION TIP: You can use rice, quinoa, or regular couscous instead of pearl couscous without changing the cooking time.

- 1 tablespoon extra-virgin olive oil
- 1 garlic clove, minced
- 1 cup fresh or frozen corn kernels
- 2 cups cherry or grape tomatoes, halved
- 1½ cups pearl couscous
- 2½ cups vegetable broth or water
- ½ tablespoon freshly squeezed lemon juice
- Zest of 1 lemon
- 1 tablespoon chopped fresh parsley
- ½ teaspoon kosher salt
- ¼ teaspoon freshly ground black pepper

1. Select SEAR/SAUTÉ on your Ninja® Foodi™ and set the temperature to HI. Select START/STOP to begin. Let preheat for 5 minutes.

2. Pour the olive oil into the pot. Once the oil is hot, add the garlic, corn, and tomatoes and sauté for 1 minute. Select START/STOP. Mix in the couscous and pour in the broth.

3. Assemble the pressure lid, making sure the pressure release valve is in the SEAL position. Select PRESSURE and set it to HI. Set the time to 1 minute. Select START/STOP to begin.

CONTINUED ▶

Corn and Tomato Couscous continued

continued

STORAGE: Store in airtight containers in the refrigerator for up to 4 days or in the freezer for up to 1 month.

4. When the cooking is complete, allow the pressure to release naturally for 10 minutes. After 10 minutes, quick release the remaining pressure by moving the pressure release valve to the VENT position. Carefully remove the lid when unit has finished releasing pressure.

5. Add the lemon juice, lemon zest, and chopped parsley, and season with the salt and pepper. Stir to combine.

Per serving: Calories: 223; Total fat: 3g; Saturated fat: 0g; Cholesterol: 0mg; Sodium: 105mg; Carbohydrates: 42g; Fiber: 3g; Protein: 7g

Butternut Squash Mac and Cheese

SERVES 6

Macaroni and cheese is always a family favorite. I love making all sorts of variations, especially some that sneak more veggies into my family's meals. In this recipe, the butternut squash cooks with the macaroni, and once you start mixing in the milk and cheese, the vegetable softens into a puree and becomes one with the cheesy sauce.

NUT-FREE, UNDER
30 MINUTES

PREP TIME: 10 minutes
TOTAL COOK TIME:
14 minutes

APPROX. PRESSURE
BUILD: 10 minutes
PRESSURE COOK:
3 minutes
PRESSURE RELEASE:
quick

SAUTÉ: 1 minute

STORAGE: Store in airtight containers in the refrigerator for up to 4 days or in the freezer for up to 1 month. Stir in a bit of milk or butter before reheating.

1 tablespoon extra-virgin olive oil

½ small onion, diced

1 garlic clove, minced

1 teaspoon kosher salt

½ teaspoon paprika

1 pound elbow macaroni

2 cups peeled and cubed butternut squash

3½ cups chicken broth

1 cup milk

1½ cups shredded cheddar cheese

1 tablespoon unsalted butter

1. Select SEAR/SAUTÉ on your Ninja® Foodi™ and set the temperature to HI. Select START/STOP to begin. Let preheat for 5 minutes.

2. Pour the olive oil into the pot. Once the oil is hot, add the onion, garlic, salt, and paprika and sauté for 1 minute, just until the onion and garlic are fragrant and soft. Select START/STOP.

3. Place the macaroni in the pot, then top with the butternut squash. Pour in the chicken broth and gently push down on the pasta and squash to submerge them in the liquid.

4. Assemble the pressure lid, making sure the pressure release valve is in the SEAL position. Select PRESSURE and set it to HI. Set the time to 3 minutes. Select START/STOP to begin.

CONTINUED ▶

5. When the cooking is complete, quick release the pressure by turning the pressure release valve to the VENT position. Carefully remove the lid when the unit has finished releasing pressure.

6. Stir in the milk, cheese, and butter until the cheese has melted and the butternut squash is fully incorporated in the sauce.

Per serving: *Calories: 486; Total fat: 16g; Saturated fat: 8g; Cholesterol: 40mg; Sodium: 841mg; Carbohydrates: 66g; Fiber: 4g; Protein: 20g*

Beet Salad with Citrus and Feta

Beets are definitely having a moment in the food world. From beet juice to beet chips, I love all the different ways these vibrant, hearty vegetables are finding their way into our diets. Honestly, I wasn't always a fan of beets—until I had a beautiful beet salad at one of my favorite restaurants. The Foodi™ does a great job of cooking beets just until they are fork tender, bringing out their sweetness.

GLUTEN-FREE, NUT-FREE, ONE AND DONE, VEGETARIAN

PREP TIME: 10 minutes, plus 10 minutes to chill **TOTAL COOK TIME:** 30 minutes

APPROX. PRESSURE BUILD: 10 minutes

STEAM: 20 minutes **PRESSURE RELEASE:** quick

ACCESSORIES: Cook & Crisp™ basket

PREP TIP: Peeled raw beets can stain your hands, so wear gloves when cleaning and peeling them.

STORAGE: Refrigerate in airtight containers for up to 4 days.

1½ cups water

3 medium golden beets, trimmed and peeled

16 to 20 small red beets, trimmed and peeled

Ice for an ice bath

2 medium oranges, peeled, seeded, and sliced

½ small red onion, thinly sliced

½ cup crumbled feta cheese

4 cups mixed salad greens

½ cup balsamic vinaigrette

1. Pour the water into the inner pot of your Ninja® Foodi™. Lower the Cook & Crisp™ basket into the pot, then place the beets in the basket in a single layer.

2. Assemble the pressure lid, making sure the pressure release valve is in the SEAL position. Select STEAM and set it to HI. Set the time to 20 minutes. Select START/STOP to begin.

CONTINUED ▶

3. When the beets are almost finished steaming, prepare an ice bath: Fill a large glass or metal bowl halfway with ice, then pour in just enough cold water to cover the ice. Set aside.

4. When the cooking is complete, quick release the pressure by turning the pressure release valve to the VENT position. Carefully remove the lid when the unit has finished releasing pressure.

5. Using tongs or a large spoon, carefully transfer the beets to the ice bath and let them chill for 10 minutes.

6. When the beets have cooled, remove them from the ice bath and pat them dry with paper towels. Cut the beets into slices.

7. Layer the red beets and golden beets at the bottom of 6 large jars or to the side of 6 airtight containers. Layer the orange slices over the beets, then the slices of red onion, the crumbled feta cheese, and finally the greens. Seal and refrigerate. When ready to eat, toss the salad with about 2 tablespoons of dressing.

Per serving: Calories: 165; Total fat: 4g; Saturated fat: 2g; Cholesterol: 11mg; Sodium: 522mg; Carbohydrates: 31g; Fiber: 7g; Protein: 6g

Black Bean Burrito Bowl

SERVES 8

If you're ever having one of those super-busy days, this black bean burrito bowl is an excellent one-and-done recipe to make. It calls for ingredients that you most likely already have in your pantry, refrigerator, and freezer. Simply combine the ingredients in the pot, then let the Foodi™ do all the work. It's also easy for each person to customize their bowl with favorite toppings.

DAIRY-FREE, GLUTEN-FREE, NUT-FREE, ONE AND DONE, UNDER 30 MINUTES, VEGAN

PREP TIME: 5 minutes
TOTAL COOK TIME: 20 minutes

APPROX. PRESSURE BUILD: 10 minutes
PRESSURE COOK: 10 minutes
PRESSURE RELEASE: natural for 5 minutes, then quick

STORAGE: Store in airtight containers in the refrigerator for up to 4 days or in the freezer for up to 1 month. Add a teaspoon or two of stock or water before reheating. This helps fluff up the rice again while it warms up.

- 2 (14.5-ounce) cans black beans, drained and rinsed
- 2 cups frozen corn kernels
- 2 teaspoon chili powder
- 2 teaspoon ground cumin
- 1 teaspoon paprika
- 1 teaspoon kosher salt
- ½ teaspoon garlic powder
- ½ teaspoon onion powder
- 2 cups salsa
- 2 cups basmati rice
- 2 cups vegetable stock or water
- Sliced or chopped avocado, shredded lettuce, sour cream, shredded cheese, chopped fresh cilantro (optional)

1. Place the beans, corn, chili powder, cumin, paprika, salt, garlic powder, and onion powder in the inner pot of your Ninja® Foodi™. Stir to combine. Spoon the salsa on top but do not stir.

2. Spread the rice evenly over the top of the salsa, then pour the stock over the rice. Gently push down on the ingredients so they are mostly submerged in the liquid.

3. Assemble the pressure lid, making sure the pressure release valve is in the SEAL position. Select PRESSURE and set it to HI. Set the time to 10 minutes. Select START/STOP to begin.

4. When the cooking is complete, quick release the pressure by turning the pressure release valve to the VENT position. Carefully remove the lid when the unit has finished releasing pressure.

5. Scoop the ingredients into bowls and add any optional toppings, if using, such as sliced or chopped avocado, shredded lettuce, sour cream, shredded cheese, and chopped cilantro.

Per serving: Calories: 326; Total fat: 1g; Saturated fat: 0g; Cholesterol: 0mg; Sodium: 627mg; Carbohydrates: 69g; Fiber: 9g; Protein: 12g

Ninja® Foodi™ Deluxe XL Pressure Cooker
COOKING TIME CHARTS

Pressure Cook Chart

INGREDIENT	WEIGHT	PREPARATION	WATER	
POULTRY				
Chicken breasts	2 lbs	Bone-in	1 cup	
	6 small or 4 large (about 2 lbs)	Boneless	1 cup	
Chicken breasts (frozen)	4 large (2 lbs)	Boneless	1 cup	
Chicken thighs	8 thighs (4 lbs)	Bone-in/skin-on	1 cup	
	8 thighs (2 lbs)	Boneless	1 cup	
Chicken, whole	4–5 lbs	Bone-in/legs tied	1 cup	
Turkey breast	1 breast (6–8 lbs)	Bone-in	1 cup	
GROUND MEAT				
Ground beef, pork, or turkey	1–2 lbs	Ground (not in patties)	½ cup	
Ground beef, pork, or turkey (frozen)	1–2 lbs	Frozen, ground (not in patties)	½ cup	
RIBS				
Pork baby back	2½–3½ lbs	Cut in thirds	1 cup	
ROASTS				
Beef brisket	3–4 lbs	Whole	1 cup	
Boneless beef chuck-eye roast	3–4 lbs	Whole	1 cup	
Boneless pork butt	4 lbs	Season as desired	1 cup	
Pork tenderloin	2 tenderloins (1–1½ lbs each)	Season as desired	1 cup	

TIP Use hot water for pressure cooking to build pressure quicker.

	ACCESSORY	PRESSURE	TIME	RELEASE
	N/A	High	15 mins	Quick
	N/A	High	8-10 mins	Quick
	N/A	High	25 mins	Quick
	N/A	High	20 mins	Quick
	N/A	High	20 mins	Quick
	Cook & Crisp™ Basket	High	25-30 mins	Quick
	N/A	High	40-50 mins	Quick
	N/A	High	5 mins	Quick
	N/A	High	20-25 mins	Quick
	N/A	High	20 mins	Quick
	N/A	High	1½ hrs	Quick
	N/A	High	1½ hrs	Quick
	N/A	High	1½ hrs	Quick
	N/A	High	3-4 mins	Quick

Pressure Cook Chart

INGREDIENT	WEIGHT	PREPARATION	WATER	
STEW MEAT				
Boneless beef short ribs	6 ribs (3 lbs)	Whole	1 cup	
Boneless leg of lamb	3 lbs	Cut in 1-inch pieces	1 cup	
Boneless pork butt	3 lbs	Cut in 1-inch pieces	1 cup	
Chuck roast, for stew	2 lbs	Cut in 1-inch pieces	1 cup	
HARD-BOILED EGGS				
Eggs†	1–12 eggs	None	½ cup	
VEGETABLES				
Beets	8 small or 4 large	Rinse well, trim tops and ends; cool and peel after cooking	½ cup	
Broccoli	1 head or 4 cups	Cut in 1–2-inch florets, remove stem	1 cup	
Brussels sprouts	1 lb	Cut in half	1 cup	
Butternut squash (cubed for side dish or salad)	20 oz	Peel, cut in 1-inch pieces, remove seeds	1 cup	
Butternut squash (for mashed, puree, or soup)	20 oz	Peel, cut in 1-inch pieces, remove seeds	1 cup	
Cabbage (braised)	1 head	Cut in half, slice in ½-inch strips, remove core	1 cup	
Cabbage (crisp)	1 head	Cut in half, slice in ½-inch strips, remove core	1 cup	
Carrots	1 lb	Peel, cut in ½-inch pieces	½ cup	

	ACCESSORY	PRESSURE	TIME	RELEASE
	N/A	High	25 mins	Quick
	N/A	High	30 mins	Quick
	N/A	High	30 mins	Quick
	N/A	High	25 mins	Quick
	N/A	High	4 mins	Quick
	N/A	High	15–20 mins	Quick
	Reversible rack in lower position	Low	1 min	Quick
	Reversible rack in lower position	Low	1 min	Quick
	N/A	Low	2 mins	Quick
	Reversible rack in lower position	High	2 mins	Quick
	N/A	Low	3 mins	Quick
	Reversible rack in lower position	Low	2 mins	Quick
	N/A	High	2-3 mins	Quick

†Remove immediately when complete and place in ice bath.

Pressure Cook Chart

INGREDIENT	WEIGHT	PREPARATION	WATER
Cauliflower	1 head	Cut in 1-inch florets, remove stem	½ cup
Collard greens	2 bunches or 1 bag (16 oz)	Remove stems, chop leaves	½ cup
Green beans	1 bag (12 oz)	Whole	1 cup
Kale leaves/greens	2 bunches or 1 bag (16 oz)	Remove stems, chop leaves	½ cup
Potatoes, red (cubed for side dish or salad)	2 lbs	Scrub, cut in 1-inch cubes	½ cup
Potatoes, red (for mashed)	2 lbs	Scrub, whole, large potatoes cut in half	½ cup
Potatoes, russet or Yukon Gold (cubed for side dish or salad)	2 lbs	Peel, cut in 1-inch cubes	½ cup
Potatoes, russet or Yukon Gold (for mashed)	2 lbs	Peel, cut in 1-inch thick slices	½ cup
Potatoes, sweet (cubed for side dish or salad)	1 lb	Peel, cut in 1-inch cubes	½ cup
Potatoes, sweet (for mashed)	1 lb	Peel, cut in 1-inch thick slices	½ cup
DOUBLE-CAPACITY VEGETABLES			
Broccoli	2 heads or 8 cups	Cut in 1- to-inch florets, remove stem	1 cup
Brussels sprouts	2 lbs	Cut in half, remove stem	1 cup
Butternut squash	48 oz	Peel, cut in 1-inch pieces	1 cup
Cabbage	1½ heads	Cut in half, remove core	1 cup
Green beans	2 bags (24 oz)	Whole	1 cup

*The time the unit takes to pressurize is long enough to cook this food.

	ACCESSORY	PRESSURE	TIME	RELEASE
	N/A	Low	1 min	Quick
	N/A	Low	6 mins	Quick
	Reversible rack in lower position	Low	0 mins*	Quick
	N/A	Low	3 mins	Quick
	N/A	High	1–2 mins	Quick
	N/A	High	15–20 mins	Quick
	N/A	High	1–2 mins	Quick
	N/A	High	6 mins	Quick
	N/A	High	1–2 mins	Quick
	N/A	High	6 mins	Quick
	Deluxe Reversible Rack (both layers)	Low	1 min	Quick
	Deluxe Reversible Rack (both layers)	Low	1 min	Quick
	Deluxe Reversible Rack (both layers)	High	3 mins	Quick
	Deluxe Reversible Rack (both layers)	Low	5 mins	Quick
	Deluxe Reversible Rack (both layers)	Low	0 mins*	Quick

Pressure Cook Chart

INGREDIENT	AMOUNT	WATER	
GRAINS			
Arborio rice*	1 cup	3 cups	
Basmati rice	1 cup	1 cup	
Brown rice, short/medium or long grain	1 cup	1¼ cups	
Coarse grits/polenta*	1 cup	3½ cups	
Farro	1 cup	2 cups	
Jasmine rice	1 cup	1 cup	
Kamut	1 cup	2 cups	
Millet	1 cup	2 cups	
Pearl barley	1 cup	2 cups	
Quinoa	1 cup	1½ cups	
Quinoa, red	1 cup	1½ cups	
Spelt	1 cup	2½ cups	
Steel-cut oats*	1 cup	3 cups	
Sushi rice	1 cup	1½ cups	
Texmati® rice, brown**	1 cup	1¼ cups	
Texmati® rice, light brown**	1 cup	1¼ cups	
Texmati® rice, white**	1 cup	1 cup	
Wheat berries	1 cup	3 cups	
White rice, long grain	1 cup	1 cup	
White rice, medium grain	1 cup	1 cup	
Wild rice	1 cup	1 cup	

	PRESSURE	TIME	RELEASE
	High	7 mins	Natural (5 mins) then Quick
	High	2 mins	Natural (5 mins) then Quick
	High	15 mins	Natural (5 mins) then Quick
	High	4 mins	Natural (10 mins) then Quick
	High	10 mins	Natural (10 mins) then Quick
	High	2–3 mins	Natural (5 mins) then Quick
	High	30 mins	Natural (10 mins) then Quick
	High	6 mins	Natural (10 mins) then Quick
	High	22 mins	Natural (10 mins) then Quick
	High	2 mins	Natural (10 mins) then Quick
	High	2 mins	Natural (10 mins) then Quick
	High	25 mins	Natural (10 mins) then Quick
	High	11 mins	Natural (10 mins) then Quick
	High	3 mins	Natural (10 mins) then Quick
	High	5 mins	Natural (10 mins) then Quick
	High	2 mins	Natural (5 mins) then Quick
	High	2 mins	Natural (5 mins) then Quick
	High	15 mins	Natural (10 mins) then Quick
	High	2 mins	Natural (5 mins) then Quick
	High	3 mins	Natural (5 mins) then Quick
	High	22 mins	Natural (5 mins) then Quick

*After releasing pressure, stir for 30 seconds to 1 minute, then let sit for 5 minutes.

**TEXMATI is a registered trademark of Riviana Foods, Inc. Use of the TEXMATI trademark does not imply any affiliation with or endorsement by Riviana Foods, Inc.

Pressure Cook Chart

INGREDIENT	AMOUNT	WATER	
LEGUMES			
All beans, except lentils, should be soaked 8 to 24 hours before cooking.			
Black beans	1 lb, soaked 8–24 hrs	6 cups	
Black-eyed peas	1 lb, soaked 8–24 hrs	6 cups	
Cannellini beans	1 lb, soaked 8–24 hrs	6 cups	
Cranberry beans	1 lb, soaked 8–24 hrs	6 cups	
Garbanzo beans (chickpeas)	1 lb, soaked 8–24 hrs	6 cups	
Great northern beans	1 lb, soaked 8–24 hrs	6 cups	
Lentils (green or brown)	1 cup dry	2 cups	
Lima beans	1 lb, soaked 8–24 hrs	6 cups	
Navy beans	1 lb, soaked 8–24 hrs	6 cups	
Pinto beans	1 lb, soaked 8–24 hrs	6 cups	
Red kidney beans	1 lb, soaked 8–24 hrs	6 cups	
This section does not require beans to be soaked.			
Black beans	2 lbs	4 quarts (16 cups)	
Black-eyed peas	2 lbs	4 quarts (16 cups)	
Cannellini beans	2 lbs	4 quarts (16 cups)	
Cranberry beans	2 lbs	4 quarts (16 cups)	
Garbanzo beans (chickpeas)	2 lbs	4 quarts (16 cups)	
Great northern beans	2 lbs	4 quarts (16 cups)	
Lima beans	2 lbs	4 quarts (16 cups)	
Navy beans	2 lbs	4 quarts (16 cups)	
Pinto beans	2 lbs	4 quarts (16 cups)	
Red kidney beans	2 lbs	4 quarts (16 cups)	

	PRESSURE	TIME	RELEASE
	Low	5 mins	Natural (10 mins) then Quick
	Low	5 mins	Natural (10 mins) then Quick
	Low	3 mins	Natural (10 mins) then Quick
	Low	3 mins	Natural (10 mins) then Quick
	Low	3 mins	Natural (10 mins) then Quick
	Low	1 min	Natural (10 mins) then Quick
	Low	5 mins	Natural (10 mins) then Quick
	Low	1 min	Natural (10 mins) then Quick
	Low	3 mins	Natural (10 mins) then Quick
	Low	3 mins	Natural (10 mins) then Quick
	Low	3 mins	Natural (10 mins) then Quick
	High	25 mins	Natural (15 mins) then Quick
	High	25 mins	Natural (15 mins) then Quick
	High	40 mins	Natural (15 mins) then Quick
	High	40 mins	Natural (15 mins) then Quick
	High	40 mins	Natural (15 mins) then Quick
	High	30 mins	Natural (15 mins) then Quick
	High	30 mins	Natural (15 mins) then Quick
	High	30 mins	Natural (15 mins) then Quick
	High	30 mins	Natural (15 mins) then Quick
	High	40 mins	Natural (15 mins) then Quick

Air Crisp Chart for the Cook & Crisp™ Basket

INGREDIENT	AMOUNT	PREPARATION	
VEGETABLES			
Asparagus	1 bunch	Cut in half, trim stems	
Beets	6 small or 4 large (about 2 lbs)	Whole	
Bell peppers (for roasting)	4 peppers	Whole	
Broccoli	1 head	Cut in 1–2-inch florets	
Brussels sprouts	1 lb	Cut in half, remove stems	
Butternut squash	1–1½ lbs	Cut in 1–2-inch pieces	
Carrots	1 lb	Peeled, cut in ½-inch pieces	
Cauliflower	1 head	Cut in 1–2-inch florets	
Corn on the cob	4 ears, cut in half	Whole, remove husks	
Green beans	1 bag (12 oz)	Trimmed	
Kale (for chips)	6 cups, packed	Tear in pieces, remove stems	
Mushrooms	8 oz	Rinse, cut in quarters	
Potatoes, russet	1½ lbs	Cut in 1-inch wedges	
	1 lb	Hand-cut fries, thin	
	1 lb	Hand-cut fries, soak 30 mins in cold water then pat dry	
	4 whole (6–8 oz)	Pierce with fork 3 times	
Potatoes, sweet	2 lbs	Cut in 1-inch chunks	
	4 whole (6–8 oz)	Pierce with fork 3 times	
Zucchini	1 lb	Cut in quarters lengthwise, then cut in 1-inch pieces	

	OIL	TEMP	COOK TIME
	2 tsp	390°F	8–10 mins
	None	390°F	45–60 mins
	None	400°F	25–30 mins
	1 Tbsp	390°F	10–13 mins
	1 Tbsp	390°F	15–18 mins
	1 Tbsp	390°F	20–25 mins
	1 Tbsp	390°F	14–16 mins
	2 Tbsp	390°F	15–20 mins
	1 Tbsp	390°F	12–15 mins
	1 Tbsp	390°F	7–10 mins
	None	300°F	8–11 mins
	1 Tbsp	390°F	7–8 mins
	1 Tbsp	390°F	20–25 mins
	½–3 Tbsp canola	390°F	20–25 mins
	½–3 Tbsp canola	390°F	24–27 mins
	None	390°F	35–40 mins
	1 Tbsp	390°F	15–20 mins
	None	390°F	35–40 mins
	1 Tbsp	390°F	15–20 mins

Air Crisp Chart for the Cook & Crisp™ Basket

INGREDIENT	AMOUNT	PREPARATION	
POULTRY			
Chicken breasts	2 breasts (¾–1½ lbs each)	Bone-in	
	2 breasts (½–¾ lb each)	Boneless	
Chicken thighs	4 thighs (6–10 oz each)	Bone-in	
	4 thighs (4–8 oz each)	Boneless	
Chicken wings	2 lbs	Drumettes & flats	
Chicken, whole	1 chicken (4–6 lbs)	Trussed	
Chicken drumsticks	2 lbs	None	
BEEF			
Burgers	4 quarter-pound patties, 80% lean	1-inch thick	
Steaks	2 steaks (8 oz each)	Whole	
PORK & LAMB			
Bacon	1 strip to 1 (16 oz) package	Lay strips evenly over edge of basket	
Pork chops	2 thick-cut, bone-in chops (10–12 oz each)	Bone-in	
	4 boneless chops (6–8 oz each)	Boneless	
Pork tenderloins	2 tenderloins (1–1½ lbs each)	Whole	
Sausages	4 sausages	Whole	
FISH & SEAFOOD			
Crab cakes	2 cakes (6–8 oz each)	None	
Lobster tails	4 tails (3–4 oz each)	Whole	
Salmon fillets	2 fillets (4 oz each)	None	
Shrimp	16 jumbo	Raw, whole, peel, keep tails on	

	OIL	TEMP	COOK TIME
	Brushed with oil	375°F	25–35 mins
	Brushed with oil	375°F	22–25 mins
	Brushed with oil	390°F	22–28 mins
	Brushed with oil	390°F	18–22 mins
	1 Tbsp	390°F	24–28 mins
	Brushed with oil	375°F	55–75 mins
	1 Tbsp	390°F	20–22 mins
	None	375°F	10–12 mins
	None	390°F	10–20 mins
	None	330°F	13–16 mins (no preheat)
	Brushed with oil	375°F	15–17 mins
	Brushed with oil	375°F	15–18 mins
	Brushed with oil	375°F	25–35 mins
	None	390°F	8–10 mins
	Brushed with oil	350°F	8–12 mins
	None	375°F	7–10 mins
	Brushed with oil	390°F	10–13 mins
	1 Tbsp	390°F	7–10 mins

Air Crisp Chart for the Cook & Crisp™ Basket

INGREDIENT	AMOUNT	PREPARATION	
FROZEN FOODS			
Chicken nuggets	1 box (12 oz)	None	
Fish fillets	1 box (6 fillets)	None	
Fish sticks	1 box (14.8 oz)	None	
French fries	1 lb	None	
	2 lbs	None	
Mozzarella sticks	1 box (11 oz)	None	
Pot stickers	1 bag (10 count)	None	
Pizza Rolls	1 bag (20 oz, 40 count)	None	
Popcorn shrimp	1 box (16 oz)	None	
Tater Tots	1 lb	None	

	OIL	TEMP	COOK TIME
	None	390°F	11–13 mins
	None	390°F	13–15 mins
	None	390°F	9–11 mins
	None	360°F	18–22 mins
	None	360°F	28–32 mins
	None	375°F	6–9 mins
	Toss with 1 tsp canola oil	390°F	11–14 mins
	None	390°F	12–15 mins
	None	390°F	8–10 mins
	None	360°F	19–22 mins

MEASUREMENT CONVERSIONS

VOLUME EQUIVALENTS (LIQUID)

US Standard	US Standard (ounces)	Metric (approximate)
2 tablespoons	1 fl. oz.	30 mL
¼ cup	2 fl. oz.	60 mL
½ cup	4 fl. oz.	120 mL
1 cup	8 fl. oz.	240 mL
1½ cups	12 fl. oz.	355 mL
2 cups or 1 pint	16 fl. oz.	475 mL
4 cups or 1 quart	32 fl. oz.	1 L
1 gallon	128 fl. oz.	4 L

OVEN TEMPERATURES

Fahrenheit (F)	Celsius (C) (approximate)
250°F	120°C
300°F	150°C
325°F	165°C
350°F	180°C
375°F	190°C
400°F	200°C
425°F	220°C
450°F	230°C

VOLUME EQUIVALENTS (DRY)

US Standard	Metric (approximate)
⅛ teaspoon	0.5 mL
¼ teaspoon	1 mL
½ teaspoon	2 mL
¾ teaspoon	4 mL
1 teaspoon	5 mL
1 tablespoon	15 mL
¼ cup	59 mL
⅓ cup	79 mL
½ cup	118 mL
⅔ cup	156 mL
¾ cup	177 mL
1 cup	235 mL
2 cups or 1 pint	475 mL
3 cups	700 mL
4 cups or 1 quart	1 L

WEIGHT EQUIVALENTS

US Standard	Metric (approximate)
½ ounce	15 g
1 ounce	30 g
2 ounces	60 g
4 ounces	115 g
8 ounces	225 g
12 ounces	340 g
16 ounces or 1 pound	455 g

INDEX

ACKNOWLEDGMENTS

This cookbook came to life with the help of many amazing people. Thanks to the Rockridge Press and Ninja® Foodi™ teams—you've been wonderful to work with! Special thanks to my editor Cecily McAndrews for her keen eye and fantastic suggestions; I learned so much from you. Thanks to my parents, Lina and Marlowe Jayme, and my brother, David Jayme, for always believing in me and for being my biggest cheerleaders. Big love to my Lola Epyon, who, along with my mother, taught me the joy of cooking for others. Thanks to my husband, Alain, for being the calm in my storm, and to my awesome kids, Ethan and Cate. I love you all so much and appreciate your always honest taste-testing. Finally, I want to express my immense gratitude to dear friends, family, and blog readers for your support over the years. You are the reasons I continue to cook and create. Thank you!

ABOUT THE AUTHOR

 **Marlynn Jayme Schotland** is a food, wine, and travel blogger and photographer with more than 15 years of experience in the food and wine industry. She shares recipes, food and wine pairings, and food and wine travel guides on her blog, UrbanBlissLife .com. She is also a recipe developer and consultant for food and beverage brands, and her recipes have been featured on *The Drew Barrymore Show*, *O, The Oprah Magazine*, *Shape*, *Good Housekeeping*, and more. As a mom of two teenagers, she strives to create delicious, elevated, everyday recipes and easy-to-follow meal plans that any home cook can make in less time, with fewer dishes and a whole lot of love.

CPSIA information can be obtained
at www.ICGtesting.com
Printed in the USA
JSHW052051170521
14858JS00003B/3